ENGLISH TRAGEDY I

A Picture of Shakespeare's Tragedies

ENGLISH TRAGEDY I

A Picture of
Shakespeare's Tragedies

❧

Robert Marchant

EDGEWAYS

copyright © 1984, 2003 The Brynmill Press Ltd

first published 1984
by
The Brynmill Press Ltd
Pockthorpe Cottage, Denton, Harleston
Norfolk IP20 0AS England

first paperback edition 2003

typeset by the publishers in Linotype Granjon
using the kerned f ligatures

I.S.B.N. hard covers 0 907839 08 8
I.S.B.N. paper covers 0 907839 71 1

British Library Cataloguing in Publication Data: a catalogue record
of this book is available from the British Library.

The right of Robert Marchant to be identified as the author of this
work has been asserted by him in accordance with the Copyright,
Designs and Patents Act 1988.

All Brynmill publications are unsubsidised.
www.edgewaysbooks.com

CONTENTS

Acknowledgements

I am very grateful for criticism and advice to Professor C. I. E. Donaldson, Mr F. H. Langman, Mr Ian Robinson, Miss Julia Robinson, Mr D. L. Sims and Mr Terence Watson. My greatest debt is to Miss Adrienne Steadson for a great deal of work in formulating tough-minded and sensitive criticism from which I hope I have benefited.

Acknowledgement is made to the Editor of *Philosophical Investigations* and Basil Blackwell Ltd for permission to use here the material under "The Idea of the Tragic".

R. F. M.

The Text

Shakespeare is quoted from The Works of Shakespeare edited by John Dover Wilson, Cambridge University Press, occasionally emended (between pointed brackets, < ... >) from the First Folio.

to

Adrienne Steadson

ἡ γὰρ τραγῳδία μίμησίς ἐστιν οὐκ ἀνθρώπων ἀλλὰ πρά-
ξεων καὶ βίου [καὶ εὐδαιμονία καὶ κακοδαιμονία ἐν
πράξει ἐστίν, καὶ τὸ τέλος πρᾶξίς τις ἐστίν, οὐ ποιό-
της· εἰσὶν δὲ κατὰ μὲν τὰ ἤθη ποιοί τινες, κατὰ δὲ τὰς
πράξεις εὐδαίμονες ἢ τοὐναντίον]· οὔκουν ὅπως τὰ ἤθη μι-
μήσωνται πράττουσιν, ἀλλὰ τὰ ἤθη συμπεριλαμβάνουσιν
διὰ τὰς πράξεις· ὥστε τὰ πράγματα καὶ ὁ μῦθος τέλος
τῆς τραγῳδίας, τὸ δὲ τέλος μέγιστον ἁπάντων.

CHAPTER I

The Idea of the Tragic

For tragedy is a representation, not of man, but of actions and of life; the good or evil condition of men lies in action; and the *telos* is an action, not a characteristic. " The way people are " means their make-up; whether they are good or happy or the opposite means what they do. It is not in order to represent the human characteristics that performances are put on: characteristics, rather, are what are assumed in the dramatic performance of actions; since the deeds or story is the *telos* of tragedy, the *telos* being the most important thing.

——Aristotle, *de Arte Poetica Liber*, 1450a, 16–23 (author's translation)

Aristotle, in the above passage, is defining tragedy by its *telos*, which he says is to depict, not sorts of people, but actions and life. What people are and what they do are not of course separable, nor does Aristotle suggest that they are—he speaks of the actions of people, which means actions having an identity. He is concerned to say, not that human characteristics are one thing and actions another, but rather that to set out to depict the one (as your *telos*) is not the same thing as to set out to depict the other. If your *telos* is to depict human actions and life, it is presupposed in this that you will depict people who are a certain way—people of a certain make-up, and disposition and so forth, such as the actions show. There is a clue in what he says here that is worth following out irrespective of what he may say elsewhere in the *Poetics*. The hint he gives is that if a tragedy is of its essence a representation of actions and the life made in them, the tragic itself is going to have essentially to do with the nature of actions and the life made in them. " The nature of actions " is really what is in question: what relation do the consequences of an action bear to its nature, for instance? If the question is what is tragic about a representation of actions, it is going to have to do with asking what actions they are; with characterizing actions, rather than with scrutinizing them for their agent's make-up and thus explaining them.

To characterize an action in a drama is not to show, on the grounds of the action, what its agent is like, and it is not to show (by implication from this) the action as arising from what its agent is like: each of these means merely to show what human intelligibility the action possesses. To characterize it is not to show its congruence with what its agent is like or what has gone before, but to show what manner of action it is. It is to show the unique life brought to pass as this particular action. A drama depicts actions, not in the light of characteristics, that is, but in the light of particular things done—or rather, "doing". It depicts them as things their agent is particularly about; things he creates; things that proceed from him and what he is doing. Since everyone at least agrees in calling only terrible things tragic, tragedy may be inferred to mean something terrible that somebody is about or creates, or that proceeds from somebody and what he is doing. Tragedy is, at least, a "creating" that is terrible.

To behold a creating that is terrible is to wonder at what the characters in a tragedy do. As will appear, this wonder is essential. To wonder at what they do in a sense means to ask a question; yet, if it comes from wonder, our asking a question cannot all the same mean our inquiring into the causes of what they do. For if it is aroused by a representation of actions and of life our wonder arises as much out of their acting for reasons that are apparent as out of the results. It is wonder and not puzzlement. It may be useful to reflect that not everything that comes to expression as a question of the form, "why is this happening?" or "why has this happened?" must be a desire to know what caused something to come about. This can be seen by considering the example of the question, "why has this happened?" as it can be asked by someone grieving over a bereavement: we can see that he may not be asking for an explanation or a hypothesis, for this would not help. He may be seeking rather to come to terms with a difficult fact that has entered his life, and with which life itself now confronts him differently. Nor need his question be a rhetorical one, if in putting it he is not adopting an attitude towards anything but rather seeking to recognize life as it now appears.

Such questions do not seek and are not satisfied by explanations, but rather they lead to recognitions. The term *tragic* will appear upon examination to be no explanation of anything and not to belong to the asking of answerable questions, but instead to the comprehension of a world, or picture of how things can go. As a term of art it belongs to the comprehension of dramatic events as constituting a picture, or view of how things can go, of something specific, say love. One picture, that is: for if we call a work of art tragic this can be shown to go necessarily with recognizing in the events that it depicts a uniquely constituted world. This uniqueness is inherent in the concept of a representation of actions and of life. If happiness or goodness is a matter of what people do, it means that, with respect to a tragic representation of things people do, the world of the tragedy means the protagonist's tragic world that he brings to pass as he acts. *Tragic* does not explain his bringing it to pass, but is in the nature of a verdict on his humanly intelligible actions and the life that is to be seen in them.

The verdict that an event is tragic does not explain it, but is a form of comprehension of it: it can stand in the place of mere incomprehension of the actions comprizing it, and of whatever suffices to show they are coherently a man's actions and not nonsense. But is the tragic not always identified with events of a certain form? It is normally found in events of a certain form, perhaps, but it may be questioned whether it can denote events having a certain form. A given form of events can be represented trivially as well as profoundly, for example, and as will appear this is a distinction not in degree but in kind. Where events are represented, say, as constituting a chapter of misfortunes, the representation gives a different picture of how things can go from what is given where events are represented, say, as brought about in an unavoidable way unique to their agent. Where the term *tragic* is used to denote events having a certain form, things different in kind (in the above examples, misfortunes undergone and catastrophes unavoidably brought about) are being subsumed under one category, that of a literary *genre*. This has its use, but the use is a minor application of the term *tragic*. The difference in question is not a difference in the artist's understanding of something objective which he contemplates, but a difference in conception: a difference not in the "presentation" of events, but in what events are conceived. This means that where events having a certain form are called tragic, unless it is merely to denote the *genre* to which they belong, they are called tragic, not on account of their form, but on account of the character of events they are. This has to do with what might be termed their seriousness: how deep it goes with their agent to perform the actions he does.

If what is tragic in this non-categorical sense is the character of events, not their form; and if a work of art be defined as possessing coherence; this tragic character must belong to all the parts of a tragedy and not just to some of them. This gives the clue to which of these examples of kinds of event can be called tragic. The development in the events of a tragedy will no doubt be from a propitious to a calamitous state of affairs; but if it is to possess coherence the represent-ation must be of a tragic sequence, not a sequence "become tragic", say by things' having fallen out for the worst. This means that the worsening in a tragic action is something in-trinsic in the whole business coming to the full. What is tragic in the action of a tragedy, then, cannot enter it intermediately or the action would constitute not a tragedy, but a hybrid. If it is a tragedy the actions and their psychological intelligibility together with the calamity to which they lead, are expressions of a world. They are expressions of a world constituted by a development that is not accidental, but intrinsic in the nature of the actions making up its events. The nature of the devel-opment in the events is, in fact, the "world" or sense of things that the action of the tragedy expresses. A chapter of misfor-tunes could not exhibit this coherence (of something intrinsic in the nature of all its parts coming to expression) without ceasing to be a mere chapter of misfortunes. The misfortunes would cease to be mere misfortunes to the extent to which they exhibited this coherence. Unless they were participated in rather than passively undergone they would be arbitrary and capable of expressing nothing but their arbitrariness: but if they were participated in they would to that extent be the creation of their participants. The worsening would then exhibit the coherence of something intrinsic in the nature of the actions coming to expression, and the " misfortunes " be none. They would exhibit a terribleness peculiar to human actions, and the coherence of a tragic sequence and not one " becoming tragic " or one merely chaotic. This is not merely to argue that tragedies cannot be chapters of misfortunes: the example serves to bring out an essential feature of the tragic, namely that it exhibits a terribleness peculiar to human actions, to things people do.

The tragedy, it was inferred, has to do with the " something terrible " that is taking place where we use the term. It can now be seen that the terrible thing is not the state of affairs produced in upshot of the actions but the nature of the actions, and the consistency of their upshot with their nature. *Tragic* recognizes a terrible kind of creating, to which kind the actions are seen as belonging all along, and not just in the event. What is tragic about the development in the actions therefore lies in the nature of their agent's will. What he comes to do is seen as belonging to what he is doing all along in a way that makes us regard what he is doing all along with awe. If a tragedy consists in a doing or a creating (a *praxis*), and depicts in it a life; and if what is tragic is a " worsening " intrinsic in the nature of the depicted actions; then a tragedy is the expression of a life, the sense of which, or whose nature, is this intrinsic nature of its depicted actions. What are we to say where the acts of will creating the sense or nature of a life are intrinsically terrible, but that their agent is subject to a form of necessity? It depends on what is meant by necessity. If he is subject to necessity, the necessity can only lie in his acts of will and not behind them, as it were causing him to perform them. What is terrible is the spectacle of his performing intrinsically terrible acts of will. Our terror is in fact at his inability not to perform them, as will be explained. Many things cannot be avoided and there is nothing terrible about it, but it is " a pity ", or " a terrible shame ", or a " tragedy " in the usage of the newspapers: if his acts of will strike the beholder with terror it cannot be because he cannot avoid them merely. An inability that resides in the cause is not terrible in the way an inability that resides in the character of his actions is. What is terrible to see is an unavoidable kind of willing, and that not only is it unavoidable, it is not accidental: it exhibits the singular nature of the agent. That is the tragic kind of necessity. There is no explanation " why " he cannot avoid willing his actions beyond the recognition of the human singularity that this constitutes. That is what is terrible and constitutes the tragic picture.

A world conceived tragically is one in which things are shown to " come by necessity ", in the old phrase. The analysis of the tragic is the analysis of the sense in which the protagonist of a tragedy is said to do what he does of necessity.

Necessity cannot describe the production of action out of character, as has sometimes been thought, or out of "identity", as Professor Goldberg's definition of fate implies that it can:

It is not moral " character " that is fate so much as identity— the particular limits that enable a being to think and feel and will at all. And it is not so much " fate " in the ordinary sense of the word, as the limited possibilities of our common world that are " chosen " by a particular self . . . those possibilities of our common life that seem to reach out for a particular form in which to realize themselves.

——S. L. Goldberg, *An Essay on " King Lear "*, Cambridge University Press, 1974, p. 85

Goldberg here equates a man's fate with the life made in what he does, but he sees his making the life to be seen in his actions only in terms of its psychological mechanism (fate equals identity equals " those possibilities of our common life that seem to reach out for a particular form in which to realize themselves "). But fate identified with " the particular limits that enable ... " dispenses with necessity and hence, as has been shown, with tragedy. *Character* meaning the sort of man he is or *identity* meaning the nature of his psyche and its needs relative to " the limited possibilities of our common world " can necessitate nothing: they only describe the human intelligibility of the actions he in fact performs. *Identity* is not the explanation of actions called tragic, but the thing to be comprehended as tragic. If a man obeys promptings of his psyche, yet he might not have obeyed them. If he obeys them, that may be something he does, not something that happens to him. Where it is seen as happening to him, so that his make-up is seen as causing him to perform the actions in which his identity is dramatically realized, we are doing psychology and he is being regarded in the light of a case. If necessity belongs to the nature of tragedy, character or " identity " cannot be adduced as explaining actions called tragic.

It is perhaps worth remarking here that " character in action ", the idea which Professor Goldberg is criticizing, is ambiguous. A character in a drama constitutes a human reality or life in being the way his actions show him to be (a dramatic identity is the human intelligibility of actions in a drama). If we speak as though he must behave as he does, being the kind of man we can see in his actions (and so forth) we import an illegitimate " must " and illegitimately use of him the language of cause and effect or of explanation. If on the other hand we do not, but drop the " must ", we are left with Professor Goldberg's " particular self " choosing among limited possibilities of self-realization in order to fulfil its needs (" in order to " being the implication in his phrase, " reach out for a particular form in which to realize themselves ")—left, that is, speaking a language of cause and effect entailment still. To call the protagonist a tragic protagonist is indeed to say of him that he has to behave as he does; only that is not to explain him; it is to describe him. Goldberg might want to retort that he, too, is describing him, i.e. as " reaching out for a particular form ": that is who " he " is. The crucial distinction to draw is that though what we describe him as being is intelligible (in the ways Goldberg sees), it is inexplicable. The tragedy is not the psychological intelligibility of the actions but the picture given by the intelligible actions. With respect to the human being the protagonist is (the tragic nature that appears in what he does), there can be no " because ". The tragedy is the depiction of a human being whose psychic needs (if that is what is in question) are realized unavoidably: and not only is it unavoidable, it is not accidental. The tragic protagonist is conceived as unavoidably creating the world or sense of things his actions constitute; not as falling into doing so (which would deny that he creates his world and leave us with accidents, not actions), and not as seizing upon possibilities in a merely characteristic way.

"Character in action" can serve so long as the suggestion of causation that it can convey is disallowed, namely the suggestion that the character, make-up or identity of a dramatic personage in some sense causes him to perform the actions in which it is realized. *Identity* elaborates his actions (in fact their conveying an identity is a condition of our understanding them at all), but does not cause him to perform them. With this suggestion disallowed, the phrase can express the idea that the character of a dramatic personage means the character of his actions, or what we might term the human coherence they exhibit. But then, this will not explain *necessity* since, as has been said, *identity* is not an explanation of anything but a species of description. The actions a dramatic personage performs constitute a human reality—that is their sense: but their sense cannot explain why he performed these actions and not some others, equally intelligible in terms of his character and the world he inhabits, or any at all. What must be said further to its meaning the human coherence of his actions is that in a tragedy the human coherence in question is more than a matter of the actions' adding up to a man, his psyche and its needs.

A tragedy expresses a human life whose nature is that of the unavoidable will exhibited by the actions in which it is brought to pass. The necessary character of the protagonist's creation of his world is internal to what he is about, a character that, as he goes about it, he creates. Necessity is not what causes him to create anything, but what he creates.

Necessity stands to the actions in which it is seen, not in the relation of cause to effect, but in the relation in which the picture given stands to the picture that gives it.

Character in tragedy is not psychic make-up, but will, expressed as destiny. The tragic protagonist, as he grasps what comes to him and makes it his own, determines his nature finally to the possibilities he thus creates. The action of a tragedy is thus, not a product of the man and the world in which he moves, but an essential feature of the protagonist's world. A tragedy is not a picture of " a tragedy " (i.e. of a product), but a tragic picture. To speak of a tragedy is not to specify the contents of a representation but to characterize the picture it is.

The tragic will is a will obeying not reason or even desire, in so far as desire presumes assent, but rather the self-determination of a human nature. But the important distinction to keep here is that the tragic as such shows no general truth—as it might be, that self-determination is inherent in being a human nature—but on the contrary: for the very singularity of the tragic protagonist's nature lies in its necessity to determine itself to its truth. His nature is this singular necessity. A picture of a human nature as having to determine itself to its truth, for good or evil and despite everything, is a tragic picture. The inexplicable necessity that is the tragedy is not a proof or a demonstration of anything, but a picture of things.

The intelligible but inexplicable passion, elation or despair in the tragic protagonist's actions constitutes the last judgement upon him, as it shows his actions to be actions he wills and cannot avoid willing. The nature of this " cannot " is the crux of the matter. There is no explanation of why he cannot avoid willing his actions, because that he cannot avoid it is the picture being given, the human reality depicted as the actions. Explanation can only further elaborate the essential nature of his actions. The question " why can he not avoid willing his actions?" does not ask for and could not be answered by an explanation. It belongs to the recognition of a picture of things.

CHAPTER II

Hamlet has Bad Dreams

Hamlet, his imaginative being determined by conceptions of the world's beauty and the nobility of the mind, comes to an untenable fastidiousness. He must make the evil that faces him as much his own (i.e. of his world) as he makes the beauty. The necessity is intrinsic in what beauty and nobility prove to mean as he grasps or fails to grasp a sense in things. The speeches he utters and the actions he performs exhibit an irresistibility, and the impossibility that they constitute for his life is of his own creation. He yearns after " the beauty of the world " (as he calls his father), and, holding to the love he pictures in this, repudiates love. He finds himself faced, in Claudius's desire for the crown and to possess his brother's wife and in her acquiescence, by such mean facts of desire as threaten to render null or merely contingent to himself his own deepest attachments. His father's ghost tells him that Claudius, man and king, does not represent all that love and sovereignty should amount to, but far from helping, this leads Hamlet only to suffer a sort of ecstasy. The Ghost tells him what his fastidiousness desires to hear, but leaves him with conceptions with which he can do nothing. Again, the impossibility of accomplishing anything in the language the Ghost uses is one discovered by Hamlet, a fact of his life, as he tries to act and speak. The impossibility is peculiar to the life Hamlet makes. He is inalterable in believing that the nullity he is confronted by in the marriage of Claudius and Gertrude can only be an aberration from the human. " You cannot call it love," because if this is the love of man and woman then the inevitable determinations of Hamlet's imaginative being are nothing essentially human. They are predilections of his. But Hamlet can as little retire upon private notions (which would be to own them ungrounded in the way the world is constituted) as he can confront the inadmissible facts so as to acknowledge them as belonging to the constitu-

tion of things. He is driven, and by his own desire, against
incorrigible facts; and what is noble in him (in the sense of
not to be "enlightened" by the ethos of Elsinore) twists to
abuse. He "sends up" his comprehension of "the beauty
of the world". He pretends to be mad, seeking a futile liberty
to "set it right". Discovering none, he comes in an ecstasy
to spread destruction about him, and neither from choice nor,
as he tries to believe, from election to duty, but in an indirection that exhibits a tragic intransigence.

The gentlemen of the watch see a ghost, Hamlet his beloved
father, "not two months dead", risen from the grave to accost
him. But the thing is in every instance horrible, and it is not
its "likeness to the king" that "harrows" Horatio "with
fear and wonder". Even as Barnardo holds his companions
with his atmospheric story of how it appeared the supernatural
erupts to break his spell. Horatio gathers the self-possession
to challenge it as a usurper of nature, the peace, and the person
of the dead king but it has nothing to say to this, but "stalks
away." The king is unmistakable and the Ghost incontrovertible, but the fact of the apparition is an obscure one that
challenges understanding. The sentries' fear, however, departs
with the Ghost; and when Horatio declares that "in the gross
and scope of [his] opinion / This bodes some strange eruption
to [their] state" the invitation to relate it to the national
emergency is readily taken up and they "sit down" to dis-
burden themselves. Horatio's reflections upon ghosts, like
Banquo's on witches, recognizes that this does not speak to
him and that its horror will remain particular. So he looks
to Hamlet.

In aloof attendance on the new king, Hamlet is given to
witness the spectacle of a politician, and no consummate one,
setting his tradesman's hand to the moulding of a public
occasion. The political inanities—"defeated joy ... an aus-
picious, and a dropping eye ... wisest sorrow"—however, come
forth with a notable absence of front. What might in the
circumstances have exhibited the control of a performance
shows instead an untrembling smoothness, and Claudius, con-

fident and unapprehensive of his effect, looks in his natural
element, uttering political inanities. His dispositions are quite,
quite happy and as free of ill-will or apprehension as of regal
power or command (compare " Meantime we shall express
our darker purpose. / Give me the map there. Know ... ").
He does not come over as the uninteresting, official type his
language might as easily have sorted with, but there is a false
note. An efficiency which extends to the ready disposal of
" incumbent " grief for your brother belongs to a peculiarly
unmeaning will. The very absence of embarrassment carries
a suggestion of *hubris*. He oversteps the bounds of what political expediency permits: " it us befitted / To bear our hearts
in grief ... ." Hamlet's rejoinders to this show more of disdain for ill-breeding than of opposition to anything masterful.
And when Gertrude loyally echoes Claudius's representations
to Hamlet, her courtly phrases (" Do not for ever with thy
veilèd lids / Seek for thy noble father in the dust ") and ele-
gance of sentiment (" Thou know'st 'tis common, all that
lives must die, / Passing through nature to eternity ") are
saved from triteness only by a certain sadness and by not being
meant unkindly. In Gertrude's words the absence of unease
seems to bespeak an emotional suspension; and if Hamlet
does not answer her with the "unforced accord" that Claudius
says " sits smiling to [his] heart," he does answer her. We
can, however, see what his " for I have that within which
passes show " hits at.

What he has within him which " passes show " he seems
able only to project, in a youthful way, on to dissatisfaction
with court duplicity, the emptiness of mourning shows which
" indeed seem, / For they are actions that a man might play."
The distinction he draws between being and seeming, though,
looks less of a banal and merely disgruntled one as the King
turns all Hamlet's trouble to arguments, which he proceeds
to settle in front of the court. (The false note in Claudius's
assurance and assumption of a style of " mature common
sense " is struck most noticeably here as, incompetently, he
entreats Hamlet to remain at court.) Parental instruction
forms itself as readily in his mouth and as much as though
" to the manner born " as does state direction:

> It shows a will most incorrect to heaven ...
> as common
> As any the most vulgar thing to sense,
> Why should we in our peevish opposition
> Take it to heart? fie, 'tis a fault to heaven ... .

Claudius does not play the king, but is the King, and what-ever goes with it. His untroubled facility means only that he is equal in a quite untroubled way to being the King. It is without even covert malice that he is able to conclude:

> Madam, come.
> This gentle and unforced accord of Hamlet
> Sits smiling to my heart.

The bland assumption bears Gertrude along. But if she seems in a dream, Claudius looks fascinated by the glib logic of his role.

If Hamlet bears himself as one who finds himself up against life; and not so much in simple, private disaffection with it as out of an utterly thwarting realization of what the world he inhabits proves to be; it is not merely from peculiarity of char-acter that he might. The " weary, stale, flat and unprofitable uses of this world " he does not conceive as cause of the dis-may he feels, but as root and branch with his dis-may, the world unutterable and he unworthy. No satisfaction lies for him in noting that before him, and unquestionably of the world, is Claudius's clockwork simulacrum of royalty that embodies a cynicism so little conscious of itself as hardly to amount to anything so robust. What Hamlet cannot re-cognize lightly is that at the centre of the glib king ticks the vitally uninterested will merely to shove into another's place. His own passion of dismay contrasts with such a will to make the torment it would cause him unignorable. The degree of tiresomeness is that there can be no new thing under the sun if that is all there is to the way of the world. If even after a suspicious death (" foul deeds will rise ... ") and a hasty marriage with a nasty name, the sum of events should be such a nothing of politic blandness and neuter instrumentality, well, the nose turns at it, then

Fie on 't, ah fie, 'tis an unweeded garden
That grows to seed, things rank and gross in nature
Possess it merely.

Hamlet knows of Claudius only that he cannot stomach him.
His mother he sees as gross in her consent to such a man's
offers. Yet Gertrude appears simple and incurious rather than
" rank and gross in nature ". Hamlet twists away from the
bland facts of a world inimical to fineness, into disaffection.

His imagination turns now here, now there, blindly impelled
by a need simply to lay hold on some real object of belief.
He seizes in his dead father upon the notion of a god-like man:

So excellent a king, that was to this
Hyperion to a satyr, so loving to my mother,
That he might not beteem the winds of heaven
Visit her face too roughly—heaven and earth
Must I remember?

In his father, solicitous that the " winds of heaven " should
not spoil his wife's pale beauty, he pictures to himself the
blossom on humanity. Whatever his picture's limitations (if
it shows the blossom on humanity), the inspiration in it shows
subsequently as counterpart in Hamlet of the way he is mad-
dened by what is between Claudius and Gertrude and driven
to want its mere annihilation. It is counterpart in the end of
the way his oath by " heaven and earth " (and later hell)
accompanies his destruction. The passion in Hamlet, that is
to say, is necessarily circumscribed, bound to what this man
knows and is able to reach. It is because of the desire in
which he invests such conceptions as this that Hamlet finds
what is between Claudius and Gertrude not so much dis-
tasteful as what his soul must refuse (to employ a phrase of
Job's*). And it is because of the necessarily limited, and for
that very reason truly human, desire in such conceptions that
the impulsion powerfully but obscurely present in his talk of
" things rank and gross in nature " is a tragic one, eventuating

---

* "The things that my soul refused to touch are as my sorrowful meat."
—Job vi. 7, Authorized version

in the disaster of his sexual revulsion, and his death. The tragedy is a matter of the unavoidable desire by which he brings it about. In Hamlet's immediate, unobjectified recoil from " things rank and gross " he blames Gertrude more than he has warrant for, but the reaction we come to see as a gesture of the love of this man. What " love " means in his limited inspiration cannot also mean (for him, as he realizes it) Claudius's wanting and Gertrude's absentee consent.

Nevertheless, there it is: while

> she would hang on him [the senior Hamlet]
> As if increase of appetite had grown
> By what it fed on.

There is an irreducibility to this protestation of Hamlet's. In the expression, he discovers the finality—for him—of a *sine qua non* for love. And as what he says and does proves possible or impossible, his comprehension of love assumes the character, not of a predilection, but of a form of desire. The difficulty that, as desire, it constitutes for his life is portended here by the fervency with which he protests it. Protesting a necessity for him, Hamlet is undeniable; but to protest it is not to obey it; and where Hamlet is faced with obeying it, or staying true to the nobility in it, in what he has to do about his father's murder, desirous belief and attachment are brought inevitably to the judgement of the genuineness of actions. He attempts to reason his revulsion and to speak the language of a conventional code, but it only comes out unconvincing: " O most wicked speed ... to post / With such dexterity to incestuous sheets!" Disapproval of the speed; disapproval of Gertrude's marrying her deceased husband's brother—these turn after all on adult common sense. He cannot hit it, and concludes lamely: " it is not, nor it cannot come to good." He cannot draw poison to the surface of what he contemplates so as to draw it off, because it is poison in what he contemplates only as it works in Hamlet himself; and it works in him to determine and to incapacitate his will. So in monstering his mother with "incest"—investing the term in Greek horror —he is able only to satisfy a gathering fury of impotence.

The real intimations of catastrophe are the ones betrayed by Hamlet's preoccupation as he casts about ostensibly to ascertain the facts. It is with his mind already upon his father ("'A was a man, take him for all in all, / I shall not look upon his like again ") that he is informed of the Ghost; and he is not astonished and incredulous, but troubled and thought-struck: "Indeed, indeed sirs, but this troubles me ... 'Tis very strange." He seems to be startled only by the form the revel-ation takes; and taken aback to find his obscure unease so spectacularly confirmed (the uncomfortable misgiving recurs). He resolves to speak with the Ghost in terms of resolving to brave hell: "though hell itself should gape / And bid me hold my peace." He will confront what negates his sense of life; but it can only be in the recognition that it must undo him. Conceiving it thus, he conceives his mother's and Claudius's desire as an aspect of a world with which, to his horror, his own is root and branch. For he is to brave what he must not merely judge but embrace as real.

Their world is envious of Hamlet. Laertes tells his sister on parting from her to hold the "trifling" of Hamlet's "favours" "a fashion, and a toy in blood" and not to "open" her "chaste treasure ... / To his unmastered import-unity." With his own, conventionally sanctioned importunity he sees corruption where there is only lack of conformity to the conventional sophistication of the court. He takes her innocence for simplicity. Ophelia gives Laertes as good as she gets ("you yourself shall keep the key of it"); but then Polonius parades his cynicism before her as though she ought to applaud, and Ophelia has to endure in her father's wit at the expense of Hamlet's "tenders of affection" to her a base indifference to herself.

It is not so much that the ethos of Elsinore is one inimical to and contemptuous of passion or real feeling that revolts Hamlet, as the recognition to which he is forced, that the world of Elsinore is of the world. As he waits for the ghost of his father to walk he discourses on the way court swagger detracts from "the pith and marrow of our attribute" with courtier-like civility enough. For all of which, his address to it when it appears is pitched in terror. He wills himself to

address in it all that it horribly seems: " I 'll call thee Hamlet, /
King, father, royal Dane." For his desire to learn the facts is
grounded deeper in him than upon suspicion of their nature.
He comprehends not a possibility, but an absolute in the duty
to put himself at the spirit's disposal unconditionally. And
that has perforce to sort with the wrong constituted by the
Ghost's apparition, " against the use of nature ". It revolts
any coherent sense of things itself; and Hamlet, determined
as he is to hear words of his father's from the apparition's
mouth, uses of it a figure of vomiting:

> O, answer me!
> Let me not burst in ignorance, but tell
> Why thy canonised bones, hearsed in death
> Have burst their cerements? why the sepulchre,
> Wherein we saw thee quietly inurned,
> Hath oped his ponderous and marble jaws
> To cast thee up again?

Hamlet so far accommodates himself to this violation, recalling
the funeral of his father and using " we " and " thee " to it, as
to allow the Ghost to speak to him in the way it only can to
him. His language, however, displays the violence of the
need. His words are shaken from him in the terror, not of a
ghost alone, but of a peculiar portent for his life. The Ghost
leads him " apart " only by Hamlet's own, intrinsically apprehensive desire. But his address to it is full of the courage of
his apprehension:

> What may this mean
> That thou, dread corse, again in complete steel
> Revisits thus the glimpses of the moon,
> Making night hideous, and we fools of nature
> So horridly to shake our disposition
> With thoughts beyond the reaches of our souls?
> Say why is this? wherefore? what should we do?

Horatio does not have Hamlet's vulnerability to " thoughts
beyond the reaches of our souls " or dread of them, but he is
(as L. C. Knights says, *An Approach to " Hamlet "*, p. 47)

choric in warning Hamlet that it does not malignly overcome
him and bring him to destruction. Horatio responds to just
what leads Hamlet to cope with such thoughts, declaring "my
fate cries out" as he keeps off his anxious companions with
his sword.

The Ghost indeed "finds [him] apt." He is inspired, and
eager that his inspiration should be invested in the substance
of action:

> Haste me to know't, that I with wings as swift
> As meditation or the thoughts of love,
> May sweep to my revenge.

It finds him apt; but already, as he is willing agent, Hamlet is
willing victim of the course it proposes. He is possessed by a
passion that sets its sights far beyond the Ghost's merely
offended shot. The Ghost is disarmingly straightforward and
solemnly requires of Hamlet that he do his duty and redress
the wrongs done his father:

> duller should'st thou be than the fat weed
> That rots itself in ease on Lethe wharf,
> Would'st thou not stir in this.

It is not because he is dull but on the contrary, because of his
desirous anticipation of the Ghost ("O my prophetic soul!"),
that Hamlet is in the event of its confirming his suspicion unable to stir. His very attraction to vengeance conceived as
duty comes, in Hamlet, from a deep inoperancy in respect of
the Ghost's language. When the Ghost speaks of Hamlet's
father's mortal enemy the style in which it accuses Claudius
characterizes an ethos which for Hamlet were "devoutly to be
wished":

> Ay, that incestuous, that adulterate beast,
> With witchcraft of his wits, with traitorous gifts,
> O wicked wit and gifts, that have the power
> So to seduce … .

The Ghost, seeing as sinner the abuser of wits and gifts, the employer of witchcraft and the power to seduce, does not see, but comprehends under a conception of cause and effect, the human facts that drive Hamlet to a frenzy because they are not to be explained away. With respect to Claudius's and Gertrude's desires, why and wherefore are neither here nor there; their desires are merely as different from what Hamlet imagines in " he would not beteem the winds of heaven / Visit her face too roughly " as they are opposite to anything in which he can acknowledge life to consist. Hamlet does not find himself up against the villain of the Ghost's conception. His " what should we do?" is an unanswerable question.

The Ghost is gallant. It views Gertrude in a sympathetic light, showing a cast of mind something akin to her own simplicity and a pragmatic nobility radically unlike Hamlet's. It is full of dismay at Gertrude's sad lapse of taste:

> ... won to his shameful lust
> The will of my most seeming-virtuous queen;
> O Hamlet, what a falling-off was there!
> From me whose love was of that dignity,
> That it went hand-in-hand even with the vow
> I made to her in marriage, and to decline
> Upon a wretch whose natural gifts were poor
> To those of mine.

It is not in a jealous fury but grieved at her unchastity, sad for her and filled with anger at Claudius's getting away with " shameful lust ". It took only a Claudius to scuttle such uprightness. Hamlet would follow his father's lights; yet he is only able to see that love as dismayingly indefinable. When later he does follow the Ghost and seeks to reprehend Gertrude's immorality (" Leave her to heaven, / And to those thorns that in her bosom lodge / To prick and sting her "), he is reduced to abuse. His words betray that he cannot believe in her guilty conscience but feels himself confronted in her by something short of human. The Ghost's sad reproachfulness shows greater acumen than this, recognizing Gertrude's absence from anything high and damnable and speaking of a lapse of discernment.

Hamlet seizes in fact upon the Ghost's clear conception, " to decline / Upon a wretch" in eagerness to have it so simple. The effort of will requisite to his undertaking vengeance shows in the determined glee of his pact with the Ghost and macabre humour with his companions. In his haste to place himself out of their reach there shows anxiety to pursue a clear objective, cost what it might. Anxious determination is transparent too in his conviction that "the time is out of joint, O cursed spite, / That ever I was born to set it right!" It is in such a forced and energized state alone that he can go on.

To put Ophelia from him is the cruel concomitant of the device he settles on for going on. Herself, Ophelia answers her father's query, "Mad for thy love?" wonderingly, struck by events and assenting to Polonius's suggestion: "My lord, I do not know, / But truly I do fear it." She fears, that is, for Hamlet, that he might indeed be mad as her father suggests. Polonius, who slanders her with "lust" out of indifferent habit of mind, in obedience to a new objective of easing Claudius's discomfiture over Hamlet's insanity transfers his slander of superficial and thoughtless comprehension to "love". But something really in Hamlet makes him strangely hit the target:

> This is the very ecstasy of love,
> Whose violent property fordoes itself,
> And leads the will to desperate undertakings,
> As oft as any passion under heaven ... .

He is right in seeking his advantage to smell danger in Hamlet, and love does now in one sense master Hamlet's will, bound now as it is to the realization of his inspiration in vengeance.

Claudius sets Rosencrantz and Guildenstern on to sound Hamlet out with an expediency immediately caricatured by Polonius, shamelessly mocking his daughter's affections for his advantage with the King. Their instincts are of a kind:

for duplicity, automatic and indifferent to prompting. But the voice of natural affection has here an affected drawl—" But look where sadly the poor wretch comes reading "—(Gertrude being herself taken in by Hamlet's " reading " ...), and the layers of duplicity on duplicity shows the trap that Hamlet's engagement with life here, however detached and ironical he would have it, must be. He assumes madness as much for the liberty it affords him as for the ploy—liberty, in that at least he can utter words and make gestures, even if not, strictly speaking, say or do anything. In such " mad " mimicry Hamlet can be both the noble soul fastidious of a world characterized by a Claudius and the avenging fury that will punish Claudius: but only so. Hence: " You cannot, sir, take from me anything that I will more willingly part withal, except my life, except my life, except my life." He does not so much mean this (i.e. say anything by it) as pose saying it, haunted by the meaning it lies beyond his grasp to express. He is held in an inertia of posing.

It proves intrinsically impossible for this man in this world to do anything with the language to which he is inspired. The difficulty his language makes for him comes where saying has to mean doing. The facts as Hamlet can only formulate them deny not just his tastes, but him, as their creator. If Hamlet kills Claudius in the exaction of vengeance, it makes his life insufferable in the sense that his life denies itself. " O God! I could be bounded in a nutshell, and count myself a king of infinite space; were it not that I have bad dreams ": the " thinking " that " makes good or bad " is the judgement that resides in the character in which things are said and done. The judgement to which Hamlet's spirit commits him is of an impossible nature, and his moral constitution, as it is realized by him, proves his fate. His " bad dreams " portend the inevitability with which he must discover the reality of things for him. In a world of bad heart, in which evil itself desponds, little more than something trivial related to wanting, for Hamlet to enclose himself within his imagination of the god-like in humanity would be for him to accede, abjuring action that exhibits judgement, to a base reality. Claudius may have sold his soul for the throne but he sits down to what he has bought.

He is not so much an evil will as a mindless object, evil only as it is placed and set in motion where it is.

"Revenge" is a dream of action whose language Hamlet attempts in vain to speak. He tries to display before Rosencrantz and Guildenstern a noble indifference, something of the Courtier's *sprezzatura* vis-à-vis the beauty of the world, the nobility of the mind and his own seriousness. However, his sincerity takes fire; he falls with facility into impassioned declamation and, from disgust at the facility, as readily into simple disdain: "and indeed it goes so heavily with my disposition ... ." As though his disposition were no affair of his, a mere property; the wonder of things, too, an accident of how you happen to look at it; he intimates that for all the difference that his discernment makes, it had just as well be: "this goodly frame the earth, look you, this brave o'erhanging, this majestical roof, fretted with golden fire: why, it appears no other thing to me, than a foul and pestilent congregation of vapours." Just that he can so readily encompass the world's beauty with words and invest his soul's truth in the beauty of poetry makes beauty and truth a word. The pose of noble indifference is available, after all, only to his expressive mockery. Not the thing he poses saying in this, but the posing, his mimicry of reason, is his soul speaking out:

> What a piece of work is a man! how noble in reason!
> how infinite in faculty! in form and moving how express
> and admirable! in action, how like an angel! in appre-
> hension, how like a god! the beauty of the world, the
> paragon of animals; and yet to me what is this quint-
> essence of dust? Man delights not me; no; nor woman
> neither! though by your smiling you seem to say so.*

* The First Folio is followed throughout this speech, with exclamation marks substituted for its question marks. The Second Quarto (and the Cambridge Shakespeare) has: "What a piece of work is a man, how noble in reason, how infinite in faculties, in form and moving, how express and admirable in action, how like a god &c." But man's faculties are few, while his faculty or aptitude for action is unbounded; his bearing and motions are hardly infinite, although they may be express (i.e. determinate) and then they may be admirable; angels are agents; gods are all-seeing: the Second Quarto pointing sacrifices these particularities for generalities ("how like a god!").

He is bitter and mocking about having to have man eternal
and incorruptible—a "necessity" which can amount to facile
word-spinning—and finds himself in an *impasse*, the nature he
proves to be, set over against a blandness.

A sort of cold-fish wanting has the weight of the murder of
a brother and "incest". How is he to "oppose, and end"
that? His desire, in truth, is not to murder Claudius but to
wipe him out and have the world different. Hamlet, who is
far from squeamish about killing, is fastidious, in the event,
not of committing murder so much as of living the life of
Elsinore. Claudius supplicates grace with about as much
likelihood as Hamlet talks of wreaking revenge: he is clogged
by fascination with the crown and his queen as he stretches
towards forgiveness; while Hamlet cannot contrive murder
except by—impossibly—standing outside of the frame of
things as he is only able to discover it. He makes his truth by
a recoil that he can only call cowardice:

> This is most brave
> That I, the son of a dear father murdered,
> Prompted to my revenge by heaven and hell,
> Must like a whore unpack my heart with words,
> And fall a-cursing like a very drab;
> A <scullion>! fie upon 't! foh!

He holds his hand off the avenging sword and can only see it
in a perspective of disgust. He blusters that it is too good for
Claudius to kill him at his prayers. The wonder and the
tragedy in his refusal lie in Hamlet's proximity in this to
bewilderment, as he finds himself unable but to bring himself
to where he can only withdraw from making for himself a
chaos.

Claudius sounds surprisingly like Hamlet on his own inability to be any different:

> The harlot's cheek, beautied with plast'ring art,
> Is not more ugly to the thing that helps it,
> Than is my deed to my most painted word:
> O heavy burden!

He sincerely regrets that he cannot be a king and good, and stays the same; while Hamlet, as he goes on, turns from what he discovers himself to be: he can only judge it in the terms of the best he knows. A pitiable inclination in Claudius shows by contrast a tragic necessity in Hamlet. The violence in Hamlet's language shows the pressure of him upon—and upon him of—the null world he must make his own. Claudius struggles, but only within conceptions bound to his interest. He has not, it is true, Gertrude's simplicity:

Gertrude. And for your part, Ophelia, I do wish
   That your good beauties be the happy cause
   Of Hamlet's wildness ... .
Ophelia. Madam, I wish it may:

the King wishes it may, too; as does Polonius and so forth.

   Hamlet's inability either to act (in the style his father demands) or to endure becomes the question, " to be, or not to be? " as neither alternative proves to have any reality for him. Evidently he does not have it in him to speak the language of Elsinore, call it " revenge " and assassinate Claudius; evidently he does not have it in him to abjure the world in turning away. The impossibility is exhibited by his not turning away but going on, only to arrive at disgust and frenzy. All Hamlet can end with the sword is Claudius. His contemplation of death, not as the end but as the defining limit that determines what a life is, is comparable in a sense with Cleopatra's declaration, " Die when thou hast lived," whose sense is constituted by the life she brings to pass in making it: Hamlet's tragedy lies, too, in an inspiration to utterance. His " dread of something after death, / The undiscovered country, from whose bourn / No traveller returns " exhibits, where it is spoken, dread of judgement. For Hamlet, the judgement intrinsic in action is dread: he pursues it inevitably in the sense that it is dread. He dreads life in its implicit nature, that of creation by action, and as " heaven and hell ", the poles of his mind, become the poles of his action and his life. The desire in which he moves makes for impossibility enough; the tragedy grows in his determination, within its difficulty, to apprehend with a penetrating, contracted mind, as impersonally and as free of implication as he can, so that, for instance, Ophelia cannot reach him.

The pity of this lies in her bewilderment as Hamlet disclaims her. What she is doing in acquiescing in her father's stratagem and returning Hamlet's presents is not altogether what Polonius or the King supposes. But Hamlet is not to be provoked. He will not notice her distress, but wilfully sees only the disingenuousness:

Hamlet. I loved you not.
Ophelia. I was the more deceived.
Hamlet. Get thee to a nunnery ... .

This is as much as to say, Look, you are too simple for this world. But he abuses her in groaning: "What should such fellows as I do crawling between earth and heaven?", blaming himself for imposing his unhappy complications on her simplicity. With the inappropriate reproach to himself he holds her away. He will be inviolate in his bitterness. Ophelia's emotional education is conventional, and not only does she lack Hamlet's need to further it, he is not about to recruit her. He savours bitterness: "be thou as chaste as ice, as pure as snow, thou shalt not escape calumny; get thee to a nunnery, go. ... *Ophelia.* O heavenly powers restore him!" Simply he will not have it; he will be full of grief; his soul will be disquieted: "God hath given you one <pace> and you make yourselves another, you jig, you amble, and you lisp, you nickname God's creatures, and make your wantonness your ignorance." The pettishness, as ugly as he intends, is to Ophelia an inexplicable perversity:

> O what a noble mind is here o'erthrown! ...
> Now see that noble and most sovereign reason
> Like sweet bells jangled, out of tune and harsh,
> That unmatched form and feature of blown youth,
> Blasted with ecstasy! O, woe is me!
> T' have seen what I have seen, see what I see!

Perversity it may be but Hamlet, at once cruelly putting it on and cruelly speaking his mind, now has a mind to be perverse. His necessity is to pursue an intrinsically futile liberty of action and speech; it drives him to much for which he is to blame. The tragedy resides in his being driven to such passes. Ophelia duly laments what he wilfully and falsely presents to her,

> The courtier's, soldier's, scholar's eye, tongue, sword,
> Th' expectancy and rose of the fair state,
> The glass of fashion and the mould of form,
> Th' observed of all observers, quite quite down:

he is content if she is conventionally love-lorn ("And I of ladies most deject and wretched"). His need to feel the desperation of his remedy in the ways people are affected by it, the need to have his " noble form " seen to be " blasted with ecstasy ", belongs to the humanity of Hamlet, and to the particularity of the man in which his tragedy resides. His refusal of Ophelia's love is tragic. The King senses it when he declares, " Love! his affections do not that way tend ... there's something in his soul." Hamlet's affections do not that or any other way tend precisely in that he is driven by desire.

Ophelia's distress moves Hamlet only wilfully to consign her to the company of those to whom he can say nothing. She can scarcely believe him to be " mad for [her] love ", but is bewildered. Hamlet's quipping with her at the play is unpleasant not in its indecency (it is arguably acceptable smart talk), but in its indifference to the expediency of Hamlet's being familiar with her. He uses her; and the cynicism is implicit in his will to master the dilemma he is in. When his trap with the play succeeds Hamlet is no further on, but only further in. Nor does he congratulate himself on achieving anything: he gives himself to wild exultation, mocking Rosencrantz in a wild dance of triumph. The rapturous heedlessness of what is entailed for him by Claudius's proven guilt is a recognition of sorts that Claudius's guilt means his own undoing.

He gets the taste of evil into his mouth only to savour it:

'T is now the very witching time of night,
When churchyards yawn, and hell itself breathes out
Contagion to this world: now could I drink hot blood,
And do such bitter business as the day
Would quake to look on.

The nervous force of his words belongs, not to a war dance, but to a St Vitus' dance of impotence. The conditional " could I ", making his threats portentous and stagey, only shows the impossibility of Hamlet's accomplishing vengeance. When Macbeth is on the point of murdering his king, fear is all but master of him, but:

> withered Murder,
> Alarumed by his sentinel, the wolf,
> Whose howl's his watch, thus with his stealthy pace,
> With Tarquin's ravishing strides, towards his design
> Moves like a ghost.

As Macbeth's desire for murder consummates itself and he finds the poetry of murder on his lips he knows that " he does not belong to himself" if ever protagonist did. Hamlet, faced with murdering his king, does not belong to himself (or he could) ; but he can only see it as an incapacity. To himself he seems to betray only that he is not master of himself. Where Macbeth horrifiedly comments on it as he feels himself coil into a cruel spring, Hamlet deliberately (though unavoidably) savours a horror of his stirring. The vague and unconvinced violence of intention exhibits what necessity he is under. Claudius knows that Hamlet means to murder him (the play-trick is in a language he can understand) and now repents his crime, but he finds he cannot pray " though inclination be as sharp as will ", for " whereto serves mercy / But to confront the visage of offence? " But Hamlet talks of tripping him " that his heels may kick at heaven " only to shy away, calling a sword in the back of the neck "<hire> and salary ."

He cannot acknowledge, by confronting it, the world's evil to be essential and inexterminable. He accuses his mother of

licentiousness and his stab at the arras, killing Polonius, is only
as blind a lunge. Betrayed to rage, he turns Gertrude's "O
what a rash and bloody deed is this!" back on her:

> A bloody deed—almost as bad, good mother,
> As kill a king, and marry with his brother.

The Ghost ("Hyperion") was more gallant, but then, it had
no murderous rashness to extenuate. Hamlet, subject to and
suffering the circumstances of a course of action he can neither
compass nor avoid, becomes as immoderate in his behaviour
as he accuses his mother of being:

> such an act
> That blurs the grace and blush of modesty ...
> makes marriage vows
> As false as dicers' oaths, O such a deed
> As from the body of contraction plucks
> The very soul, and sweet religion makes
> A rhapsody of words: heaven's face does glow,
> <Yea,> this solidity and compound mass
> With <tristful> visage, as against the doom,
> Is thought-sick at the act.
>
> *Queen.*   Ay me, what act,
> That roars so loud, and thunders in the index?

Hamlet cannot be reproachful and sternly just as his "duty"
requires, for what for his father was a crime against him, but
as a crime capable of being punished or avenged, must be for
Hamlet his own condemnation to a sort of hell: the world
cannot be thus constituted: "heaven's face does glow, / Yea,
this solidity and compound mass / With tristful visage, as
against the doom, / Is thought-sick at the act." The immoder-
ation of comprehending the "act" as constituting chaos
measures the intransigence of Hamlet's desirous attachments.
He cannot say what he says here temperately because the intransigence is what is getting itself expressed. He utters, not
a moral judgement, but a fact of the life that he makes. The
"thought-sickening" disintegration is the reality of the world

Hamlet possesses by acting in it—of all that "by opposing" which Hamlet makes what he is able to comprehend real. And if Gertrude's guilt has little to do with Claudius's worth and her taste (marriage vows being in question) yet Hamlet draws it thus awry, for it would be not just painful but impossible for him to answer his mother's nervously witty "Ay me, what act &c.?" with an explanation. He is "right" (no doubt it "blurs the grace and blush of modesty") but what is impossible for Hamlet is that right and wrong are not in question—as little for her as for him, could it simply come to the question. He rages against the mere discounting of the frame of things.

Vengeance might have been Hamlet's, he might have re-paid, had he only been able to conceive their love as something as deep-going as murderously passionate adultery. As he is able to conceive it, the crime presents him with difficulties of quite a different order. Hence:

> See what a grace was seated on this brow—
> Hyperion's curls, the front of Jove himself,
> An eye like Mars to threaten and command,
> A station like the herald Mercury,
> New-lighted on a heaven-kissing hill:

he thus throws her indiscrimination at his mother, not because he shares his father's sorrow at her sad lapse, but out of re-fusal of the crass, having aspect of love, possession devoid of the possibility of wonder and perhaps even of very much desire —desire, at any rate, locatable in any such order of sense as he reaches towards with his classical allusions. The indifference it is that undoes humanity, nullifies modesty and the soul of marriage and reduces religious truth to words. But Hamlet cannot just say so. He can no more speak temperately to his mother than he can render justice to Claudius. His con-ceptions find no ground in a world "thought-sick" at whose "acts" he begins to rave:

> Ha! have you eyes?
> You cannot call it love, for at your age
> The hey-day in the blood is tame, it's humble.

What maddens him is that the inability to call it love is purely his. The senior Hamlet saw it as seduction; and Gertrude does not call it anything. Hamlet throws abuse at what lies beyond reach, a nothing: he hits nothing in hitting out at the " compulsive ardour ": " Proclaim no shame / When the compulsive ardour gives the charge." But he hits out, and eventually like this:

> Nay, but to live
> In the rank sweat of an enseamèd bed
> Stewed in corruption, honeying, and making love
> Over the nasty sty.

For all his possession of the wit and self-command to mock his own seriousness ("this most excellent canopy the air, look you, this brave o'erhanging, this majestical roof, fretted with golden fire "), when seriousness becomes a matter not of perceiving but of "opposing", his poise goes. His onslaught against sex exhibits Hamlet driven from human sense by resistance on its behalf. His accidental slaughter of Polonius, which is the death of Ophelia, determines Hamlet in the mad resistance. The necessity with which he goes on in indirection shows Hamlet's subjection to the circumstances of situations of his unavoidable creation.

When Hamlet is driven to will vengeance he wills the upshot in repudiation. The more things turn out to prove his judgement right, the less are they anything he can engage with. Gertrude's inclination to confess herself touched by his accusations fades before her dismay at the spectacle presented by Hamlet as the Ghost appears to him. Her son is out of his wits. Hamlet is so evidently far indeed from the execution of his pledge that his most poignant conviction, that he must " be their scourge and minister", is a declaration allied to despair. In bidding his mother refrain from the " monster custom " in her marriage bed he is tragically pitiable. He hates Claudius, yes, because he is his mother's corrupter and his father's murderer, but also with a hatred that is not to be appeased in him.

There sharpens now a determination at least to wreak some havoc:

For 't is the sport to have the enginer
Hoist with his own petar, and 't shall go hard
But I will delve one yard below their mines,
And blow them at the moon.

" To be " is not after all so difficult ... in the one sense that
means Hamlet's disintegration. The vivid picturing of his
imagination here is " express " as Laertes's impetuous and
boyish posturing at Claudius's suggestion is. Hamlet is reduced to something akin to Laertes's " Italian " passion, with
the difference that, in Hamlet's case, it is within and as the
upshot of an inexpugnable difficulty; for Laertes this is an
available style. If Hamlet stabs now and prays later there is
nothing light and easy and Benvenuto-Cellini-like about it, but
it signifies his undoing. And now he stabs Polonius, lugs the
guts into the neighbour room, and does not reflect that they
belong to his lover's father. Only his wit attends. Now he
kindles to the fierce honour of an officer in the Norwegian
army even as he mocks at the futility of this "delicate and
tender prince " who, his " spirit with divine ambition puffed, /
Makes mouths at the invisible event."

His self-possession fails Hamlet finally at Ophelia's grave-
side, where a wild, unlocated word-play with Laertes rushes
in to fill a vacuum. Now his mockery itself fails him as a re-
fuge. Owing Laertes a real apology for his conduct, it is
beyond him: he asks his pardon in the manner of an Osric
("Who does it then? his madness. If't be so, / Hamlet is of
the faction that is wronged &c."). Ophelia possesses nothing
like Hamlet's imaginative aspiration, and nothing like his need
to ground it in reality drives her; she sees no ghost; and when
she is implicated in the circumstances of Hamlet's travail,
nothing in her experience presents itself to her as the only way
on. Her sense that her father's death and the inexplicable
decline of Hamlet are obscurely of a piece has no scaffolding
in any deep imaginative experience and amounts only to a form
of bewilderment. She goes to the death of Gertrude's aesthet-
ical elegy, though, only in the sense that Ophelia's life is cast
for her—cast in such language as that of her own " and I of
ladies most deject and wretched ". The pathos in her death

derives, not from this, but from the clear relation it bears to what Hamlet is doing and not doing; of which, whether it is suicide she commits or not, her death is the consequence. She loses her hold and becomes a living judgement on them all along with Hamlet. To the extent to which it is indeed a water-nymph ("a creature native and indued / Unto that element"), a "ministering angel", or "Frailty (thy name is woman)" who drowns, an innocence judges their various sentimentalities. It may be "very Ophelia" to distribute posies for thoughts and remembrances, but the caricature is of the woman they permit her to be. Laertes's thought of her, flower-bedecked and singing, is that her grief for their father is unbearably beautiful:

> Nature is fine in love, and where 'tis fine,
> It sends some precious instance of itself
> After the thing it loves.

He sees a touching dependence that moves him, but nothing of abandonment before a perversity of life. "Young men will do't, an they come to it" is not mere derangement, however, but Ophelia muses and sings of a love that has betrayed her love.

Ophelia handing flowers to those who will mourn her for a nymph and an angel, and singing snatches of love songs and ballads is as much given to death as Hamlet, who comes to behave as though any determinate gesture of his must prove its own denial. All he can make is a storm. A vain storm he makes with blasting word-play with Laertes in Ophelia's grave, the mockery of Laertes in his hyperbole being but wild and whirling, a mockery no longer grounded in any convinced sense of realities or possibilities. Laertes's very talk of "prettiness" ("Thought and affliction, passion, hell itself, / She turns to favour and to prettiness") contrasts with it its genuineness of feeling. His protests against the priest's misgivings as Ophelia is given only "maimed rites" are poignant for the limitations in his conventionality of expression:

> Lay her i' th' earth,
> And from her fair and upolluted flesh

> May violets spring!
>   I tell thee, churlish priest,
> A minist'ring angel shall my sister be,
> When thou liest howling.

A "picked" and artificial world, too, is guyed in the sympathetic working-man's humour of the grave-diggers; as also in the association of the "water-fly" Osric with the catastrophe of the tragedy. Hamlet's outburst of hyperbolical protestation of his love for Ophelia contrasts with this world that is a going concern to exhibit a man driven from life and sense. The Queen pronounces the performance "mere madness". But it is not that Hamlet is mad and does not live in the same world as everyone else but rather that, to the extent of taking Laertes's sort of talk to its absurd limit and to the extent of getting involved for life or death in "poison, play and duel",* he thinly and ghostly now does. He thus ends murdering the King in the suddenness of the fight.

* Alexander's phrase: Nigel Alexander, *Poison, Play and Duel* (London, Routledge & Kegan Paul, 1971)

CHAPTER III

Othello in Love

Hamlet's death is credibly his "felicity" because of the impossibility constituted by the nature of his desires; but Othello's, for the same reason, is a shameful end. The desire of each becomes a matter of his creating and suffering horrors. Hamlet, unable to come to any terms with what is between Claudius and Gertrude, can only lunge at Claudius as though to annihilate him in some way he is unable to discover. Othello's love of Desdemona is a state of grace; to find himself in this is to find himself surrendered to a light which takes from him all direction. The more complete his love for her the more impossible it is and the more he must have an end. The necessity is a compulsion upon the restless malevolence of Iago.

Othello, whether or not he is a *condottiere* supplying the demand of the mercantile city-states of Italy for soldiers (a foreigner who like the English free-lance Sir John Hawkwood of two centuries before is much esteemed by the Italians for his warlike abilities), enjoys high esteem for what Iago, with a characteristic, telling sneer at his countrymen, calls "fathom": "for their souls, / Another of his fathom they have none / To lead their business." A foreigner almost by profession, his independence is owed to his soldier's stock-in-trade of a rare personal attraction and power to command. It might have been otherwise with such a man. "Coincidence and accident," Rush Rhees writes, is

connected with ideas of destiny or of fate. And then it can be seen as characteristic of " existence in space and time ". People are born where they are—in these places, at these times and in these circumstances. What anyone learns, what he can aspire to, the friends and teachers that he finds . . . is limited by where he is, what he can reach and when he is living. And the fact that I cannot redress the worst wrongs I have done is connected with this as well.

——Rush Rhees, *Without Answers*, London, Routledge & Kegan Paul, 1969, p. 18

I cannot redress the worst wrongs I have done because I cannot stand outside of my life, to which they belong in an essential way. It is a notable fact of Othello's life that the Venetian senate that employs him is not like Elsinore, say, a mannered court whose politics fulfil the will of a king, but is the government of a republic mindful of its liberties and commanding an ideal loyalty of its citizens. Sovereign over all its citizens from the Duke down, Venice is confident and efficient where Elsinore is vitiated by sophistication and intrigue. If Elsinore has a sentimental, run-to-seed attraction towards the nobility of a Hamlet, Venice has a practical use for that of an Othello.

Like his descendant in the modern novel, Joseph Conrad's Nostromo, Othello thrives on a mystique that attaches itself to his personal authority, and as with Nostromo too there is in this an element of defence. Neither man possesses the ordinariness of a mere functionary (as does, for instance, such a luminary as the Duke of Venice), but, by a paradox, both owe their esteem to their ability in jobs. Nostromo is the mystery and legend of the Costaguanan wharves that he evidently needs to be: Othello cries "Keep up your bright swords, for the dew will rust them," and his cool authority commands the obedience due to a man of "royal siege". Yet unlike a king Othello has to remain unfathomed for his place and livelihood, and cannot become ordinary. The necessity runs contrary to his nature, and has its tragic entailment. Like Nostromo, Othello's passions are engaged and then in that practical world he finds himself in the dark, unable any longer to support the untruth of his compromised "royalty", because of Desdemona's belief in him. It is then that one of a loose, perverse will battens upon his strangeness.

Iago presents the dark side of the Venetian practicality and individualism, an opportunist, but of fierce and undetermined need. The world that can command the allegiance and consent of a Brabantio (though he dies of chagrin at his wrested consent), in Iago, whose vitality, lacking any leading positive, discharges at hazard, turns the wrong side out. In himself Iago does not appear to amount to very much; his wishes are simple and nasty; nevertheless it is such a man who here is the proving agent of great passions. He latches, with more than interest, on to the desires of whoever in his ambit is prey to them, although at one level it is an amusement—for instance to denigrate love to Roderigo as a way of feeding his love. Iago needs to believe what he tells himself when from time to time he gives himself an account of his motives in acting, but in fact the cynical offers are habitual and no less involuntary than his lewd habit of speech. For to be innocent, himself, of any deeper aim than to serve his turn, is essential to Iago's demonism; to his being the worm in the bud of Venice. He pursues Othello's destruction for no more reason than his speech runs always to low denigration—it amuses him to do as to say these things—even so the release of his savagery there is caused by the difference of Othello. The impetus of the events he is able to set in motion with such contemptuous ease itself inspires him with a conviction of their inevitability. It is an aspect of Othello's difference that this professional officer, commander in Cyprus, should be incapable of seeing what an Iago would be doing; and tragedy lies in the necessity in his maintenance of the difference. The incapacity belongs to his misplacement in that world, and to his innocence. When Othello takes Desdemona to wife it is with her desire particularly to cherish " the very quality of my lord ", and those who have a use for this " very quality " concur. But that Desdemona's " my lord " is not quite theirs possesses Iago as a fact irresistible to prove. Like Hamlet when he is pretending to be mad, Iago playing the implacable enemy of Othello does not have to dissemble very much. A salesman of attitudes, he plumes himself on his ability to say anything and intend nothing. For Roderigo he is the knowing man of the world flatteringly assuming knowingness in the other, aggrieved by the preferment before him of a " bookish spinster " in the off-hand way of one who only expected as much, and mocking Othello's grand manner: " O, sir, content you. / I follow him to serve my turn upon him ": the part is one in which he is much at home. " Whip me such honest knaves," too, is pretty much his true feeling, except as it may suggest any particular interest. He is convinced by his own fierceness that the attitude he strikes is reasonable: " Others there are / Who

... when they've lined their coats, / Do themselves homage. These fellows have some soul, / And such a one do I profess myself." Although Iago does not mind if he lines his coat, desire for gain is as nothing to his desire to hold " these fellows " who " have some soul ", along with the dutiful, in an equal disdain. He merely despises " having some soul ", which is where the amusement lies in provoking Roderigo. But if he would not " wear [his] heart upon [his] sleeve / For daws to peck at," yet he does wear his heart upon his sleeve when he makes the boast, for to know that he can fascinate such a jackdaw as Roderigo with his glitter is a necessary reassurance that he is innocent of any responsibility for what men are and do. He does not need to create fools to people the world, and it is an essential concern of Iago's to demonstrate that the world is a foolish affair without any help from him. The energy he summons to taunt Roderigo and Brabantio into raising the hue and cry after Othello, and to bustle about making sure that Othello is prepared, shows a deep anxiety that it should work all on its own. He is a wanton irritant to men's torpid wills; connects their motors to their batteries of emotion and desire and sets them going: " Call up her father, / Rouse him, make after him, poison his delight." That the requisite note can be one of his own, not particuarly assumed for the sake of his end, soothes his anxiety not to be causing all this but only, so to speak, demonstrating it.

From the moment Brabantio thrusts his night-capped head out of the upper window and demands " What is the reason of this terrible summons? / What is the matter there?" it is manifest that the irascible, important citizen is Iago's sitting duck. Iago knows he need not stint, and lays it on with relish, enjoying the filth, the old man's discomfiture, and being without parsimony the " profane wretch " Brabantio calls him:

Your heart is burst; you have lost half your soul;
Even now, now, very now, an old black ram
Is tupping your white ewe. Arise, arise.

The malice against Othello that his stratagem calls for comes out in an urgent profanity that Iago enjoys. Brabantio takes the inevitably ridiculous part, yet even so there is something quite unfunny about Iago's relish of his own outpouring that lets even Brabantio's bluster of an outraged dignitary have its dignity and pathos:

> But thou must needs be sure
> My spirit and my place have in them power
> To make this bitter to thee.

Roderigo.   Patience, good sir.
Brabantio. What tell'st thou me of robbing? This is Venice:
> My house is not a grange.

As dismay intrudes upon his sense of security Brabantio is pitiable rather than ridiculous, and when he groans "This accident is not unlike my dream," it is poignantly seen that his whole world rests firm upon just such trusted freedom of consent and responsibility as his daughter now lays claim to, to have her way despite him. The muttered expression of dismay betrays the level at which, in a man of some force and determination, his consent is given. They have "cashed" his trust, and he knows there is no redress. It goes against his nature to let it go, but he has nothing to say beyond bluster, half appealing. Desdemona has not chosen to fight her father—and that is undeniably her wisdom—for she is secure in the law. Iago knows that Othello is on certain ground, that Brabantio is beaten in advance, and that nothing he can say can make it worse for Brabantio; therefore: "you'll have your daughter covered with a Barbary horse", and "I am one, sir, that comes to tell you your daughter and the Moor are now making the beast with two backs" are simple fun for Roderigo's benefit.

Roderigo's appeal is to common prejudice: "the gross clasps of a lascivious Moor ... ". But as between "reasonable" men the racial issue needs no urging; Othello's being a soldier and a foreigner says enough. The outlandishness, the not being brought up within the rules of civility—this is only clinched by the elopement. They both speak the language of their city; Roderigo, feeling as though he has been made a fool of, says self-righteously:

> If she be in her chamber or your house,
> Let loose on me the justice of the state
> For thus deluding you.

The question, for both of them, resolves itself into an issue of civil rights and the proprieties of courtship, of behaviour in the streets and so forth, and Brabantio might as well shrug. Desdemona has given no-one just cause to stop her. She has gone to " the sooty bosom of the Moor " with no abuse of prerogative and won at Venice's own game—ironically by playing Othello's hand and defying no-one, simply taking him for her " lord " without reference to anyone else. She commits no fault they can charge her with.

It is not because he disapproves of the man that Brabantio is dismayed and bitter. Certainly Othello's power in the state weighs little against Brabantio's scope of a senator, but he feels his worth, as all do. But a part of Brabantio sees too a disaster of confident ignorance, a misfortune of erring youth too far gone to put right: " O, unhappy girl!" Something balks in Brabantio at the liberty, even though his consent to it has betrayed him in this. Although reason stays him, he is left with the feeling that Othello and Desdemona have seized a warrant which is outside his jurisdiction, and which is, infuriatingly, ratified by the ethos of Venice; he has no recourse except to insist petulantly that magic must have been used:

> Is there not charms
> By which the property of youth and maidhood
> May be abused?

A liberty with the conventions understandable given Brabantio's temperament has to be a veritable corruption of nature —his blood insists on it, as an alien form of life calmly triumphs within the citadel of its contrary.

Iago is certain that Brabantio's cause is lost, but his anxiety will not let him rest and so he puts it to Othello that the law will be invoked against him: and Othello obligingly uses the language distinctive of his difference from the world in which he moves, which tells Iago that all goes smoothly on its inevitable way:

> Let him do his spite;
> My services which I have done the signiory
> Shall out-tongue his complaints. 'T is yet to know—
> Which, when I know that boasting is an honour,
> I shall promulgate—I fetch my life and being
> From men of royal siege.

Othello lays claim to the royal prerogative confident himself that in so doing he only pictures the more vividly how they are content to have him in Venice. He assumes assent rather to the majesty of his own " life and being" than to his dues of birth and not so much that his services will be weighed with any complaints Brabantio may produce against him as that they warrant him unimpeachable, a man master of himself and taking what he wants from the world he chooses to move in:

> For know, Iago,
> But that I love the gentle Desdemona,
> I would not my unhoused free condition
> Put into circumscription and confine
> For the sea's worth.

The unfathomed world with its wealth the property of whoever dare take it is the conscious scope of this life to which love is the true centre, a great joy and consummation and, at last, a Siren's Isle. He speaks with the conviction of a man willing to have his soul put to the test:

> *Iago.* You were best go in.
> *Othello.* 		Not I; I must be found.
> My parts, my title, and my perfect soul,
> Shall manifest me rightly.

Yet he is not pronounced blameless for his " parts", but by process of law and for their usefulness to the state.

In the encounter between Brabantio and Othello, Othello's conviction of his status in the world's eyes is such that he declines to fight upon provocation, since Brabantio is his father-in-law, and the issue is past arbitrament. His easy tone is conciliatorily unprovoked:

Keep up your bright swords, for the dew will rust them.
Good signior, you shall more command with years
Than with your weapons.

Brabantio's petulant insistence on magic is foolish. Only abuse
—" the sooty bosom / Of such a thing as thou—to fear, not
to delight "—can satisfy his disarmed anger. Desdemona is
not afraid; and " fear " just betrays the check of Brabantio's
undemocratic blood at the idea of such a son-in-law. What is
obviously outraged dignity becomes an appeal to prejudice.
Brabantio is illogical; the rules he invokes are those according
to which Othello is guiltless and Desdemona judged an adult.
That " my brothers of the state / Cannot but feel this wrong
as 'twere their own " is true, but not to the point. Othello
encounters no grounds for entertaining misgivings over his
presumption of right.

In contrast with the free hand with which Othello is in
every way encouraged to conduct his affairs, the Duke of
Venice in council is shown to be very much the referee and
arbitrator: receiving despatches, requesting advice and listening
to it, deliberating upon the course of events and casting the
deciding vote in the decisions that have to be made. His
authority is diplomatic to the extent that he must pause, while
despatches arrive minute by minute from the war with the
Turks which hangs in the balance, to hear a case of abduction
involving accusations of witchcraft against his chief soldier,
upon whom his hopes depend for victory. The Duke, harassed
manager of men and affairs, readily grants Brabantio the
sympathy he claims and, glad of the excuse, lets Brabantio
present his hostages and abide by the verdict of " the bloody
book of law ". Othello can confidently predict the senate: his
assumption that he knows and is known by Venice is so borne
out that he does not scruple to address the senate in his full
native tones:

That I have ta'en away this old man's daughter,
It is most true; true I have married her:
The head and front of my offending
Hath this extent, no more.

Though it is only the need of the moment which makes him recall his life of action in " the tented field ", " till now some nine moons wasted ", that history is indeed his mainstay and claim to equity. Brabantio's confusion of Desdemona's conventionally demure bearing with " perfection ", and of the proprieties with " nature "—

> It is a judgement maimed and most imperfect
> That will confess perfection so could err
> Against all rules of nature

—carries the confident presumption of his peers' agreement that there is a case to answer, and that Othello must defend himself. But Othello does not take issue with him. He rests content with presenting himself to common judgement and the ordinary sympathies of men of the world.

Certain of this approach, he does not present himself as anything but what everyone, especially Brabantio, takes him to be, a wonder and a curiosity. Brabantio does not hate Othello, but " oft invited [him], / Still questioned [him] the story of [his] life." Othello's disarming frankness in countering Brabantio in this way is a form of innocence. He does not calculate its effect, or even behave as though he might; he sees no need to offer any other defence against Brabantio's accusations than that of reminding everybody who he is. Othello's so much more than merely professional competence in the role in which Venice has cast him prompts him reluctantly but frankly to confess the glamour of his life, yet with tenderness towards Desdemona and the ingenuousness of their courtship, so as to appeal to the senators as fellow men of the world whether she were not irresistibly innocent and eager. It is with a smile that he reveals with what a simple lure he caught her:

> She 'ld come again, and with a greedy ear
> Devour up my discourse; which I observing,
> Took once a pliant hour, and found good means
> To draw from her a prayer of earnest heart
> That I would all my pilgrimage dilate,

> Whereof by parcels she had something heard,
> But not intentively. I did consent ... .

His fondness at her artless eagerness for his stories is heightened by the recognition that was she not so artless she could not let him have a hint to cast for her:

> She gave me for my pains a world of sighs:
> She swore, in faith 't was strange, 't was passing strange;
> 'T was pitiful, 't was wondrous pitiful;
> She wished she had not heard it, yet she wished
> That heaven had made her such a man.

Othello's accurate description of Desdemona's innocent expressions of interest, surprise and wonder as invitations to woo her indeed disarms suspicion. He is perfectly what they always knew him to be. He bypasses Brabantio's ranting and the Duke—" Take up this mangled matter at the best "—is content. The fact that Othello does not feel particularly pressed to try is noteworthy.

It is left Brabantio to curse out an avowal that if Desdemona " confess that she was half the wooer, / Destruction on my head, if my bad blame / Light on the man!" Desdemona's maidenly diffidence has given way to serenity; she is both diplomatic and final:

> You are the lord of duty;
> I am hitherto your daughter. But here 's my husband.

There is no hint of gloating over the accomplished fact, only her invulnerable serenity in a great fact accomplished. Othello's own assurance, of their love and their place with one another, lets her claim her independence by right of a greater obedience: " So much I challenge that I may profess / Due to the Moor my lord." Only the absence of any sense of Brabantio's having some claim even so betrays a certain blindness and invulnerable remoteness in their union, a suggestion of *hubris*. Brabantio never reconciles himself to the fact but washes his hands of Desdemona in exasperation. He consents to nothing, but is resolute and uneasy. His refusal to accept the facts looks foolish, but his passion is no empty rage, for it kills him. Venetian civil liberty and responsibility, and Othello's way of taking what he wants and paying for it, are deeply irreconcilable. Brabantio will not bow to Othello, or to Desdemona, as she is strong in her marriage to Othello; he cries, "Please it your grace, on to the state affairs," and stays adamant. Neither will he be appeased by the Duke's diplomatic platitudes, but would sooner be discounted. His unalterable opposition to the marriage, and the lovers' unconscious opposition to him in their confident sufficiency, contrast revealingly with the senate's perfunctory interest. What Brabantio knows in his blood he does not clearly see, yet he is unappeasable in a way which is more closely related to Othello's nature than to the Duke's. Brabantio's behaviour hints at the catastrophe to come.

It does not surprise Othello to learn that he is to command in Cyprus for the Machiavellian reason that "though we have there a substitute of most allowed sufficiency, yet opinion, a sovereign mistress of effects, throws a more safer voice on you." Accepting the evaluation, he "undertakes these present wars," as an entrepreneur. When Desdemona proffers an impassioned avowal of love she is not to the point; she does not see where Othello engages them:

> That I did love the Moor to live with him,
> My downright violence and scorn of fortunes
> May trumpet to the world. My heart's subdued
> Even to the very quality of my lord.

The joyous affirmation is for Othello's and her ears. Meanwhile the world is not so inclined to raise its head at Desdemona's brave trumpet call as its solicitude to smooth the path of Othello's marriage might lead her to believe. She looks into his eyes and he into hers, uttering joyous vows superfluous to the present issue:

> I therefore beg it not
> To please the palate of my appetite;
> Nor to comply with heat <the> young affects
> In my <defunct,> and proper satisfaction;
> But to be free and bounteous to her mind.

Othello admires her brave independence, and his resolution is to give his new Italian wife the liberty her nature rises to, while Desdemona is staunch for submission, to "the very quality of my lord".

But while the senate is satisfied and the lovers have their world, Roderigo is torpid in misery. Iago dances a merry dance about him of "put money in thy purse", urging Roderigo's advantage, for he means to bleed him, and pouring scorn on sexual passion. Iago sees himself as a devil; with justice, for without some vacant soul to occupy and manipulate he is nothing:

> If sanctimony and a frail vow betwixt an erring barbarian and a supersubtle Venetian be not too hard for my wits and all the tribe of hell, thou shalt enjoy her; therefore make money. ... There are many events in the womb of time, which will be delivered. Traverse! go; provide thy money.

He has enough energy for ten mortals, yet his professed grievances and purposes are something and nothing. "Thus do I ever make my fool my purse"—perhaps: but the attraction is the fool, not the purse. Personally he is satisfied to make a picture to himself and act up to it, stagily enough:

> I have 't. It is engendered. Hell and night
> Must bring this monstrous birth to the world's light.

But his fascination with the monster is its incipient reality: Iago is dominated, despite himself, by the creative urge.

Iago, the worm in the rose of Venice, gives the lie to the leading principle of the republic. When the scene changes to a storm-beaten port in Cyprus and the "divine Desdemona" emerges from the turbulent sea to her grateful reception by Cassio as the goddess of love and consort of the hero—the hero, brave Othello, "our great captain" of war and love who "hath achieved a maid / That paragons description and wild fame"—dull civil liberty and executive responsibility are outshone by the beauty and splendour of the play's Renaissance world. Shakespeare's bright, inaccessible, self-removed Desdemona is Botticelli's clear, aerial, wind-borne Venus—in the splendour of Cassio's imagination.

Montano. What from the cape can you discern at sea?
1 Gentleman. Nothing at all: it is a high-wrought flood.

Nothing at all. The island is isolated in the cataclysmic tempest, which works a change in the blood of the play, sweeping off the strife of passion and propriety, politics and honour, sinking by a miracle the Turkish fleet and ending the wars, delivering the hero and his consort to their fair isle. It is something special:

> The wind-shaked surge, with high and monstrous mane,
> Seems to cast water on the burning Bear,
> And quench the guards of th' ever fixed pole.
> I never did like molestation view
> On the enchafed flood.

Perhaps we do not pause over the splashing of the constellations in daylight: the storm is a wonder. However he may be regarded in Venice, in Cyprus the military men look out for Othello for himself as much as for his service; Cassio rises to inspiration on the general excitement, making his friends laugh agreement with his wholehearted admiration of Othello's "achievement":

> a maid
> That paragons description and wild fame;
> One that excels the quirks of blazoning pens,
> And in th' essential vesture of creation
> Does tire the ingener.

In his willing eyes she is a miracle of beauty, humanity's blossom, *victrix* of the tempest and the Turk and visiting goddess of the precious isle. Hazards withdraw before her in her progress,

> Traitors insteeped to clog the guiltless keel,
> As having sense of beauty, do omit
> Their mortal natures, letting go safely by
> The divine Desdemona.

Thus, after the strife of Venice, in the exhilaration of the adventure, Cassio sings a laughing song of love's triumph:

> Great Jove, Othello guard,
> And swell his sail with thine own powerful breath,
> That he may bless this bay with his tall ship,
> Make love's quick pants in Desdemona's arms,
> Give renewed fire to our extincted spirits,
> And bring all Cyprus comfort.

Gallantly kissing Desdemona's fingers Cassio strolls into Iago's web, which he sets to spinning the moment he steps ashore and sniffs the island air.

Cassio's state tells Iago all he needs to know about Othello and Desdemona, confirming as actual what might have been mostly his own cynicism: they are deeply in love. The tenor of Othello's words of greeting as he clasps Desdemona justifies his sure-footed expedition. Othello sounds as though he is struggling with real disbelief, forever being taken aback to discover her:

> O my fair warrior!
>
> *Desdemona.*   My dear Othello!
> *Othello.* It gives me wonder great <,> as my content
> To see you here before me. O my soul's joy!

The wondering, pondering turn of his speech—" It gives me wonder great "—is due to a feeling too overwhelming for expression. He exclaims at his love; and it is in this vulnerable state that Iago plans to catch and hold him. For Othello is deeply moved, as though he is faced with a fulfilment so absolute he cannot secure it, but only wonder at its reality and permanence:

> If it were now to die,
> 'T were now to be most happy; for I fear,
> My soul hath her content so absolute
> That not another comfort like to this
> Succeeds in unknown fate.

His felicity takes the form of a premonition; he knows love only as a state perfect in itself and quite separate from the rest of his world. Its perfection is like a death to life—death itself could rob him of no greater bliss yet to succeed; and he takes Desdemona's gentle reassurance that it is true for a prayer that it may last:

> The heavens forbid
> But that our loves and comforts should increase,
> Even as our days do grow!

Othello.   Amen to that, sweet powers!

Othello is speechless in the face of such joy—" I cannot speak enough of this content." He is thus in a measure removed from Desdemona, and vulnerable. Compare it with the listless sensuality and elastic to-and-fro of Antony and Cleopatra's love, anything but a " content", or with Macbeth and Lady Macbeth's mutual provocation to gather fruits of horror, and Othello's absolute possession by love looks like a doom itself; the prescience in his words the reality, not Desdemona's hope for happy days. Cassio's picture of the divine Desdemona, miracle of beauty born from the sea, is his own, but the love by which he is inspired has a fragile perfection like a visionary moment. The adventure and the risk are native to Othello, but he embraces Desdemona with all his heart only to find himself bewildered and no longer the same man. He sees himself become a real lover, for "I prattle out of fashion, and I dote." Iago wonders whether Desdemona will love her soldier if he prates.

Iago, however, wastes no sublety of demonstration on Roderigo but arouses him with a display of lewd denigration, to convince him of the obvious: that it is "a most pregnant and unforced position" that Desdemona must love the Moor for " bragging and telling her fantastical lies", and that " her eye must be fed; and what delight shall she have to look on the devil? ... When the blood is made dull with the act of sport ... ." His obscenity—" blest fig's-end! ... Lechery, by this hand; an index and obscure prologue to the history of lust and foul thoughts "—reducing love to groping, automatically suggests to him a most useful cause of jealousy for himself, of Othello: " the lusty Moor / Hath leapt into my seat, the thought whereof / Doth like a poisonous mineral gnaw my inwards." The mere frenzy of expression makes it true for him; so true that, compulsively, he decides to believe that Cassio, too, has done as much for him. The fatuity would be pitiable were it not so purposeful, and the purpose so emptily malign. Iago will not recognize the seriousness in his own urgency, and disguises the compulsion under a delight in playing the villain: " 'T is here, but yet confused; / Knavery's plain face is never seen till used." When he comes round from his indulged frenzy it is to strike an attitude before an imaginary audience, in order to be reassured by its hisses of his self-mastery. Iago's personal difficulties, however, do not vitiate the effect of his indulged whims, which always obey a deeper compulsion. When Othello next has occasion to display the commander's stern demeanour, it is as Iago's dupe; doing just what Iago engineers it that he should do, his authority begins to look stricken:

> For Christian shame, put by this barbarous brawl.
> He that stirs next to carve for his own rage
> Holds his soul light; he dies upon his motion.
> Silence that dreadful bell; it frights the isle
> From her propriety. What is the matter, masters?

The disdainful assurance of "keep up your bright swords" has given way to the tones of a headmaster, mocking Othello's " perfection ".

Emilia assures Cassio correctly that Othello is well-disposed towards him—" protests he loves [him], / And needs no other suitor but his liking / To take the safest occasion by the front / To bring [him] in again." Iago understands Cassio perfectly: but the true subtlety of his understanding is to be seen in his handling of Othello. Iago is as possessed by his knowledge of Othello's nature as Othello is by love. For his ploy with Othello is not to trick him but to encourage him to feel for himself how all his native ways have turned strange to him. Because his love for Cassio would normally be sufficient reason for Othello to reinstate him Othello, in his later rebuttal of Desdemona's plea for Cassio, is acting against his own nature. Iago proceeds with the knowledge that Othello,

in the strangeness of love, will associate any unaccustomed
weakness or indecision on his own part with his love for
Desdemona; Iago sees that he need only encourage her to
exercise her "bounty" and the rest will follow. "And what's
he then that says I play the villain?" In fact he plays the
villain all the time, for the reassurance which he gains from
contempt of his adversaries. Cynically, he never takes them
on, but only marshalls them the way that they were going.
Why should the frankness of spirit that Othello loves in Desdemona not prove also to be restless, loose desire? Why should
the strong current of Othello's life, to which Desdemona
would gladly commit herself, not also be dammed by love and
burst out, to sweep all before it in a violent flood? Iago has a
nose for these cruel ironies and an itch to prove them.

His game is to be as unconsidering and unsubtle in his de-
ceptions as he dare, so as not to appear, and preferably not to
be, the cause of his victims' pain, that they may know the
worst bewildering extremity of their passion, its causeless
anguish. It is an Othello possessed by love, remote, preoccupied and suggestible, that Iago first makes notice Cassio's
attentions to his wife, with "Ha! I like not that"—an "involuntary exclamation" justifiably unsubtle, for Othello is not
listening and replies as though he had not noticed the remark:
"Was that not Cassio parted from my wife?" And Iago is
sure he need not trouble to be very ingenious:

> Cassio, my lord! No, sure, I cannot think it,
> That he would steal away so guilty-like,
> Seeing you coming.

Othello.   I do believe 't was he.

Conspicuously playing the villain, Iago finds to his pleasure
he need not pull the wool over Othello's eyes openly to mock
him. He knows that Othello is not listening but is in tune
only with Iago's implication while deaf to his words. So he
plays with him, and in Othello's absence of mind the idea of
jealousy so casually released by Iago rises like a bubble to
burst at the surface of his mind. Of course 't was he!—what
of it? But as if in a dream he drifts upon Iago's implication

and sees no question. Into love's brightness, dark beyond the peripheries, disembodied thoughts insinuate directions:

Desdemona. How now, my lord!
    I have been talking with a suitor here,
    A man that languishes in your displeasure.
Othello. Who is 't you mean?
Desdemona.   Why, your lieutenant, Cassio.

—the ponderous, militant suspicion tickles Desdemona to want to uncover this new, absent aspect of her husband and before either perceives the other's drift at all, they are sundered. Iago triumphs in his cynically elephantine style, caricaturing his own villainy under Othello's nose. All the same, it is his agency, his contrivance and his active malevolence whether he would or no that proves events. Othello's ponderous suspiciousness (" Not now, sweet Desdemon, some other time ") drops to bring Desdemona up as on a see-saw, redoubling her solicitations:

                    When shall he come?
    Tell me, Othello. I wonder in my soul
    What you would ask me that I should deny,
    Or stand so mammering on. What! Michael Cassio ... .

She is ardent as sure as fate, with all her takingness full of joyous interest in her new husband's unaccountableness. Othello is heavy and impatient, and she is full of her suit to him because he is:

    Nay, when I have a suit
    Wherein I mean to touch your love indeed,
    It shall be full of poise and difficult weight,
    And fearful to be granted.

He is irresistible to her innocent, unreserved aliveness: Othello starts to resist her.
    Wholly possessed by love, Othello becomes a bewildered, lost husband:

    Excellent wretch! Perdition catch my soul
    But I do love thee; and when I love thee not

Chaos is come again.
Iago.   My noble lord——
Othello. What dost thou say, Iago?

Awakening from the dream of love's delight, he finds—Iago,
solicitous for his honour. Love, as Othello catches a suggestion
of dissembling, begins to acquire a familiar face. If Othello
is lost it is because he knows nothing any more but where he
is now, and that is bewildering. "And when I love thee not"
means "if I should come to cease" and also "on the occasions
on which I do not". The bewilderment of love thus casts
doubt on the reality of love, present and past. Full of love, he
is aware only of it and of a darkness without it which, if he
ascribe it to the power of love over him, must be a kind of
death—and not the Christian death to life, but chaos. He
begins so to ascribe it, for what, if not love, has made him
not know how to live any more? The more it is ineffable
content the more there is something trying to burst through
the inertia of content; the something that clouds the brow of
the good Iago who is troubled for him, Othello is left to
assume. Like a false reagent, Iago proves the reality of a face
of love which unmans Othello, subduing him to its power.
It makes him and Desdemona locked adversaries; Othello avid
for the proof which he hates because it will destroy not only
him but the woman whose beauty and truth are, for him, the
last truth.

It is not because Iago is very persuasive that the confident
leader who so surely had the upper hand of a Brabantio and
the senate of Venice is in so preoccupied, suggestible a state
that the contemptuously coy insinuations of an Iago about a
Cassio sound to him horrible likelihoods. His uncertainty at
length goads him to demand that Iago speak his mind—it is
insupportable—but he is stupid, naïvely pointing out to Iago
the drift of his "musings" as though he might be missing it:
"Thou dost mean something: / I heard thee say even now,
thou likedst not that, / When Cassio left my wife. What didst
not like? &c." The dull, deliberate probing is strange in the
imperious mouth and, for its cause and his indirection,
pitiable. Iago first makes Othello jealous of him, tantalizing

him with his supposed knowledge to make him beg for confirmation, which but for stupefaction (" I cannot speak enough of this content: / It stops me here ...") were impossible to his nature:

> I'll know thy thoughts!

Iago. You cannot, if my heart were in your hand.

> Nor shall not, while 't is in my custody.

Othello. Ha!

Iago.   O, beware, my lord, of jealousy ... .

" You cannot have my knowledge." It is not with Othello as Emilia conjectures, " they're jealous for they're jealous," but he is jealous from the terror of his love's bewildering groundlessness outside itself.

Othello cannot help himself and is to blame. He thinks only to end it all. In a sense his frenzied convictions Othello half sees as such, but that cannot alter the need to keep fixed in them. Although he is wrong to entertain doubt about Desdemona's chastity he does not fall into jealousy by mistake, nor are Iago's contrivances its origin—they are its counterpart, and Othello rages at the idea of her falsity with the desperation of his need to have her true, the desperate belief in what is his life and being. He must resolve it for his life, and resolution means withdrawing his trust so that if her falseness will show, it may. Thus frankness is overborne. His love, " where he has garnered up his heart ", is as deep as his life, not an adjunct to the man he is but a profound expression of him. Her falsity means the undoing of Othello himself, the life he makes. In an obscure, unadmitted sense therefore he does want to " whistle her off and let her down the wind / To prey at fortune," for the relief. His jealousy hence comes with the finality of a decision; and hence his odd credulity of the " proof"; essentially an indifference to the proof. To think it at all is as insupportably threatening as to believe it, and anything urged against her at all is adequate to create the fatal possibility. What makes it necessary to him is his open-eyed certainty that, whatever she may be, the love here is no mistake:

> 'T is not to make me jealous

> To say my wife is fair, <feeds well,> loves company,
> Is free of speech, sings, plays and dances well;
> Where virtue is, these are more virtuous;
> Nor from mine own weak merits will I draw
> The smallest fear or doubt of her revolt;
> For she had eyes and chose me.

The absolute character of that last fact makes an inestimable difficulty for Othello, and afflicts him as it compels his wonder. Desdemona's clear, strong desire is a great certainty and grace or the merest cruel whimsy of fortune. He must be absolute, and:

> No, Iago:
> I'll see before I doubt; when I doubt, prove;
> And on the proof, there is no more but this,
> Away at once with love or jealousy!

Her self-possessed chastity confusingly filling his life makes his bliss hell. He can evidently countenance ending it, in some way he does not enquire too minutely into, but to allow that their love may amount to no more than a pleasant arrangement is impossible—" away at once " with it, then. If Desdemona is false to him there can be no healing balm of forgiveness from him because it means the spring of his life is false and unmeaning for him.

She is the bounteous, fearless Flora of his spring; and Iago helps Othello's difficult certainty (" for she had eyes, and chose me ") be his hell not by persuasion but just by harping on that very independence of spirit for which Othello loves her:

> I know our country disposition well;
> In Venice they do let heaven see the pranks
> They dare not show their husbands; their best conscience
> Is not to leave 't undone, but keep 't unknown.

Othello. Dost thou say so?

Iago. She did deceive her father, marrying you;
> And when she seemed to shake and fear your looks,
> She loved them most.

" Not to leave 't undone, but keep 't unknown " is the Machiavellian prescript translated into the private realm, and adduced not to deceive Othello but as a commonplace to which
he must assent. Of course Othello believes it of the Italians
("opinion, a sovereign mistress of effects", he is used to).
Iago does not mind, for if Othello will allow this paltry stuff,
this cheap worldly-wisdom and showy argument from Desdemona's " fear " to her " deceit ", that is his choice. Iago is
only saying (his tone claims) the common things Othello
apparently now wants to hear, though he used to interpret his
wife's wide-eyed regard differently. But if that is what he
wants, the stock of common opinion is as liberal as he can
desire:

> To seel her father's eyes up close as oak,
> He thought 't was witchcraft ... ,

Not witchcraft, though, but you-and-I know what. The low
insinuation were a bare-faced and highly improbable insult,
except that Iago is confident of saying what Othello's desperation is ready for. By just quite loosely talking, Iago makes
Othello " do dirt on himself" as he countenances the words,
as he is unable to resist doing. Othello does not attend as to
another, but assents as to the likelihood of his own imaginings.
The pregnant doubts are thrown up by musing Othello himself:

> I do not think but Desdemona 's honest.
> *Iago.* Long live she so! and long live you to think so!
> *Othello.* And yet, how nature erring from itself——
> *Iago.* Ay, there 's the rub. ...

He brings up the issue of race ("nature erring") as a niggl-
ing doubt, not a reason: Iago expresses the prejudice full-blown
and lurid for him:

> Foh! one may smell, in such, a will most rank,
> Foul disproportion, thoughts unnatural ... .

Iago has no need to argue the rank, foul and unnatural
quality of Desdemona's choice; he is not invited to express a
judgement but to speak the language of the gutter of the

Italian lady's desire for the negro. In his indifferent slander, conspicuously not persuasive in its slack foulness, Iago is cannily sure where Othello's mind is blank as to the drift of his love and life, a vacuum waiting to be filled with a horror equal to the grace he is ready to decline from. Othello in fact speaks of proof before he has been supplied with palpable reason even to suspect:

> If I do prove her haggard,
> Though that her jesses were my dear heart-strings,
> I 'ld whistle her off and let her down the wind
> To prey at fortune.

The thought that she is his to bind or loose renews his will to be master once again where he finds himself on quicksands of partnership and mutual trust, a great, uneasy joy so long as it holds him up. He loathes himself for it, but Othello sees relief ahead in loathing her:

> Haply ...
> She's gone; I am abused, and my relief
> Must be to loathe her. O curse of marriage,
> That we can call these delicate creatures ours,
> And not their appetites! I had rather be a toad ... .

That is Iago's line (to make Roderigo more besotted by his desires: "our bodies are gardens") caught up inevitably by Othello as he contemplates with fearful regard Desdemona's unconsidered mastery of her desires.

Desdemona's appetites' being for ever and from the nature of her world her own turns his joy to anguish and his magnanimous belief to hell:

> 't is the plague <to> great ones;
> Prerogatived are they less than the base;
> 'T is destiny unshunnable, like death:
> Even then this forked plague is fated to us
> When we do quicken.

Yet he knows too well upon what to retreat: "We great ones ...". Certainly his love is absolute and makes him a stranger to himself, but the sudden, total conviction and falling back upon dismay is also acquiescent. It is not the "forked plague" to which his great spirit destines him, but love—just the character of this love, makes him retire, bewildered, into unwarranted, defensive dismay:

> What sense had I, <in> her stolen hours of lust? ...
> Farewell the tranquil mind! farewell content!
> Farewell the plumed troops, and the big wars
> That make ambition virtue—O, farewell! ...
> Farewell! Othello's occupation's gone!

The monody is chanted to write himself off and keep himself fixed in his desperate certainty. The weak, dishonest posturing in his uniform ("the big wars"!) and making out he is done for prepares for Nemesis, Othello gone soft and dangerous from inequality to the unknown. His love is fatally strange, and he is in consequence guilty and to blame.

It cannot be called relief, for love cannot be switched off because it has become hell. He postures in an unconscious caricature of his old martial demeanour, no more in command of himself but tormented, and unable to see himself. "Farewell the plumed troops" is a dishonest lamentation, but anguish lies behind the self-deception of it, as it lies behind Macbeth's apostrophizing "withered Murder" to suit the horror to the deed. "Tarquin's ravishing strides" does after all accompany Macbeth's murdering strides, investing them in the sense he wants: the horrible poeticizing has that genuineness. Othello's anguish is the only centre, the only hold on reality out of which to speak, and his words do come from there although in his certitude of isolated percipience and tragic doom he is as surely mocked as Macbeth (though he at a further remove):

> If thou dost slander her and torture me,
> Never pray more; abandon all remorse;
> On horror's head horrors accumulate;
> Do deeds to make heaven weep, all earth amazed;
> For nothing canst thou to damnation add

> Greater than that.
>
> *Iago.*   O grace! O heaven forgive me!

With his downright anguish and sense of being damned himself, " destiny unshunnable ", to live in foulness aping grace and to take an unnatural vengeance which will destroy him, Othello groans in torment and suffering. Iago's always contemptuously stagey manipulations, his will that chaos should come about of itself, indeed make Othello appear not as the victim of some meaningless plot but as a great spirit tragically engaged.

Othello determines grimly and obliteratingly to have things out to their conclusion, but plainly he is stimulated by Iago's insistence on the insupportable foulness he insists is in Desdemona:

> You would be satisfied?
>
> *Othello.*   Would! nay, and will.
>
> *Iago.* And may; but how? how satisfied, my lord?
>
> Would you, the supervisor, grossly gape on—
> Behold her topped?

Othello does not have crime thrust upon him, but he pursues it: he has truck with Iago, adopting his low adversary as his evil demon, in order to prove his tragic affliction. Iago also tantalizes him with what Othello cannot himself articulate and come to terms with. Iago's satisfaction should be that Othello proves his wisdom about human foolishness, but that is strangely coupled with the feeble desire of a low nature to make others consent to lowness:

> Were they as prime as goats, and hot as monkeys,
> As salt as wolves in pride, and fools as gross
> As ignorance made drunk ... .

His wits fascinated, Othello assents to this picture of his wife's " appetites " and to being fooled by contemptuous childishness and scornfully poor stories—what Cassio said when Iago was in bed with him, and the handkerchief ploy. He is as absent from his former self as these fatuities show, yet culpable still for his acquiescence in them, and his moral collapse in the face of the difficulty made by love. The repudiation is completed only by the remorse it brings him to, which is not unqualified shame (he is not graced with that clarity) but has its exculpatory purport. The tragedy of the repudiation lies in the relation it bears to Othello's rapture, with which it is bound to him. His self-indulgence is as necessary and as obscuring as Hamlet's is, clouding repentance to the end:

> O blood, blood, blood!
> *Iago.* Patience, I say; your mind perhaps may change.
> *Othello.* Never, Iago: like to the Pontic sea,
>> Whose icy current and compulsive course
>> Ne'er feels retiring ebb, but keeps due on
>> To the Propontic and the Hellespont;
>> Even so my bloody thoughts, with violent pace,
>> Shall ne'er look back, ne'er ebb to humble love ... .

(" Now could I drink hot blood ... .") Othello gathering precipitate force to overwhelm " humble love " is more dangerous than Hamlet and more weak, mocked as he is at every step by Iago's gleeful stage villainy: " I am your own for ever." Iago solemnly scowls, and laughs up his sleeve.

Othello's " icy current and compulsive course " sounds only too like him, but his nobility is perverted. Desdemona's opinion, though wrong, is not silly: " I think the sun where he was born / Drew all such humours from him." She cannot believe that he is false to her. She lives in her wonder of him, and her faith in the nature she loves is not betrayed even when Iago has Othello where he wants him; for Iago is only able to have him where he wants him because Othello is unable, from the depth of his love, to take it any other way, to come to terms with his disappointment or to shrug off his tormentor. Othello echoes her, speaking of an old world and a new:

> A liberal hand: the hearts of old gave hands;
> But our new heraldry is hands, not hearts.

When he accuses her over the handkerchief their courtship as Othello described it to the senate is repeated with ironical exactness, only Othello now is his exotic self on purpose, not to woo Desdemona, but to mock them both and to defy her to brazen it out again. She " devours up " with a " greedy ear " his tale of an Egyptian sybil and a magic handkerchief : " Is 't possible? ... Indeed? Is 't true?"—open, curious and trusting. The more innocent she is the more convinced must he be of her power to dissemble; but if she appears simple, so does he, obeying mere Iago to the letter, suspecting his wife, and losing his temper. His compulsive suspiciousness, however, is the counterpart of her innocence: if she were brazen she could hardly matter to him. Othello is no more the simple dupe of Iago than Desdemona is simply starry-eyed. His terrible repudiation is of the woman she really is.

His need to defy her to the uttermost to face it out goes as deep as his happiness in her—and that, paradoxically, it is that changes him to a fascinated, credulous monster, somniloquently repeating childishnesses like the voice of his doom: "Naked in bed, Iago, and not mean harm?" What is he talking about, who does he think they are " who mean virtuously, and yet do so "? But of course this is not a rational voice but an exclamation at a picture which rises in his mind to make him gape and mutter of the devil and of virtue tempted. He plays a fascinated question-and-answer game with his evil demon while his judgement sleeps. When the nightmare startles him awake he is all confusion, impassioned and incoherent: " It is not words that shakes me thus. Pish! Noses, ears and lips. Is 't possible?——Confess?——Handkerchief?——O devil! [falls in a trance]." While his mind sleeps the impetus of horror bears him to the terrible, relieving conclusion: he swears and exclaims at what he uncomprehendingly finds himself to be about. The alteration in Othello is completed by Iago insulting him to his face, and he not only taking it but himself adopting Iago's style of speech:

O 't is the spite of hell, the fiend's arch-mock,
To lip a wanton in a secure couch,
And to suppose her chaste! ...
Othello. O, I see that nose of yours, but not the dog that I shall
throw it to.

His violence, and deadness to insult, are expressions only of a fixed determination which he can hardly help, nothing the less false for being involuntary, yet the falseness proceeding from the life he inevitably makes in this world with this woman.

As Othello strives with incomprehension, Desdemona's beauty and goodness rise before him: " Hang her! I do but say what she is: so delicate with her needle, an admirable musician——O she will sing the savageness out of a bear—— of so high and plenteous wit and invention——... Nay, that's certain; but yet the pity of it, Iago! O Iago, the pity of it, Iago!" The pity of the necessity, he would say. For his groans at what must be constitute his determination that what must be shall be. " The pity of it " is deeply sincere, and—as honest means upright—dishonest. Uprightness has become Othello's defence, used and made dishonourable. He would execute justice—and there he stands on the brink of self-delusion, in danger of falling forward into self-righteousness. He awakens to remorse, but meanwhile strikes Desdemona and, torment-wrung, talks like Iago. He goes but incompetently in the role Iago casts him in, speaks his lines and is stopped by them: " a subtle whore ... . And yet she'll kneel and pray; I have seen her do't." He cannot recover himself to shrug it off, but goes on, Iago's laughing-stock.

His unresolvable doubt grows hence ("There is no way but this ...") to a despair to fill the world. He envies Job his physical afflictions with deep sincerity:

> Had it pleased heaven
> To try me with affliction; had they rained
> All kinds of sores and shames on my bare head ...
> I should have found in some place of my soul
> A drop of patience. ...

" They were ashamed, because they had hoped " (Job vi. 20): it is shame in that sense to Othello that the grace of his life may prove hollow, trivial and unmeaning: his revulsion from chaos is the recoil of his human pride that is hope. But the condition of this pride is, in Othello, the extent of his recoil

—the recoil, that is, upon vengeance and vindication pursued
in the name of justice. It never occurs to Othello to turn away,
but still the only sense he can reach after is that of revenge.
His integrity can no more admit a denial of love than Hamlet's, only he is more deeply implicated as a lover and a husband than Hamlet is and it costs Othello more not to turn
away even than Hamlet's disintegration into an unwilling
avenger.

Hence arises Othello's dismay, and the wilfulness:

> But there, where I have garnered up my heart,
> Where either I must live or bear no life,
> The fountain from the which my current runs,
> Or else dries up—to be discarded thence!
> Or keep it as a cistern for foul toads
> To knot and gender in!

" There ", in his desire for Desdemona, is where he has the
only life possible to him now. Bewildered as he is and foolish
in his bewilderment, Othello manages to articulate, in this
despairing cry, his belief that to doubt love is to make life
impossible. Yet it is a despairing cry; there can be no remedy
for his doubt and the patience of Job, as that means the capacity to endure, were hardly to the point:

> Turn thy complexion there,
> Patience, thou young and rose-lipped cherubin,
> Ay, there, look grim as hell!

Hell is where Othello finds himself, and that is no posturing
but comes from the seriousness for his life of the love he is
making. The trivialization of his deep sexual passion is hell,
and Othello cannot in truth conceive Desdemona as negligibly
false. If she is a trinket she is not Desdemona: the consequence, that she should cease to be, it falls on him to conclude:

> O thou weed,
> Who art so lovely-fair and smell'st so sweet
> That the sense aches at thee, would thou hadst ne'er
>   been born!

When it is no longer his misgivings about possibilities but the actual, physical beauty of the object of his desire that makes him call her "weed", then is Othello's "moment of truth" when his love is the same thing as its impossibility and as surely as he desires her he must destroy her. If about nothing else, Othello cannot be mistaken about the seriousness of his passion.

The sense aches at her beauty still when he kills her. He is not out of love with her, but the murder of the love of his heart and his self-murder measure his love. Mercifully, he is distraught when he speaks of making a "sacrifice" in this murder. His shame demands the belief. But her beauty is wherein he has his deepest life, and indifferent nature itself must repudiate the perversion of nature that would be its trivialization:

> Heaven stops the nose at it, and the moon winks;
> The bawdy wind, that kisses all it meets,
> Is hushed within the hollow mine of earth,
> And will not hear it.

In her sexual being, ultimately, Desdemona is for Othello nature's masterpiece: "thou cunning'st pattern of excelling nature".* His wonder at her beauty measures—it is here the same thing as—his sense of the abuse.

The false note as, clinging to the belying notion of a duty, he goes to murder her, is the moral language he employs in an incantation to his resolution. Desdemona catches at this significant error:

Desdemona. No, as I am a Christian.
> If to preserve this vessel for my lord
> From any other foul unlawful touch
> Be not to be a strumpet, I am none.

---

* Cf. "Take out of [the speech] all that binds it to the story within which it occurs, and . . . the wonder at the world as well as the woman in ' Thou cunning'st pattern of excelling nature ' is now only a lecherous intriguedness. Well, it may have that aspect in the play itself, but there it is not the only one. If there is a suggestion of a commonplace pun in the first syllable of ' cunning'st ', then what is there suggested also shows as ' in narrow room Nature's whole wealth ' (*Paradise Lost* iv. 207)."—David Sims, "Scald Rymers", *The Human World*, no. 12, August, 1973

But for all his biblical reference to the body as a cistern Othello does not sound like the ghost of Hamlet's father ("O, what a falling-off was there!"), but gestures, rather, with the moralistic language only in despair of morality. Thus her answering "vessel", seizing in defence upon what she takes for his moral tone, inevitably sounds to him only like her incorrigible dissembling, now twisting his anger to arguments. He will not be answered. But it no more occurs to Desdemona than it does to him to extricate herself, and her only prayer is that they may both be forgiven: "O, heaven forgive us!" She sees there is no saving them. Desdemona's "And his unkindness may defeat my life, / But never taint my love" has the warrant that, were she less than inalterable in her love for him —more like Emilia, say, ordinarily commonsensical—she could hardly be the affliction she is upon Othello. Emilia's common sense about adultery does not make Desdemona's innocence ignorance but rather shows its goodness, which gives its sense to Othello's huge repudiation of her.

Othello has monstrously to keep himself to the point by repeating her offence to himself and maintaining that it is his duty to execute universal justice:

> It is the cause, it is the cause, my soul.
> Let me not name it to you, you chaste stars!
> It is the cause. Yet I'll not shed her blood,
> Nor scar that whiter skin of hers than snow
> And smooth as monumental alabaster—
> Yet she must die, else she'll betray more men.

Transfixed by her beauty, his ecstatic will held by the "chaste stars", he moves to the automatic conclusion. Even as he melts ("And mak'st me call what I intend to do / A murder, which I thought a sacrifice") the dishonest conviction of duty keeps him on. Love, merely, is now acknowledged by him to be as serious as murder. "Sacrifice" belongs of course with the strangely inconsequential paradox, "this sorrow's heavenly: / It strikes where it doth love." To be an agent of divine retribution is sad, but rather heavenly. The nature of what he is to accomplish begins to show through the delusion

of his intention to be a hound of heaven, and to shake
him awake, but only to a remorse tempered by a sense of
universal injustice, his need to believe in which is transparent:

> Ha! No more moving?
> Still as the grave. Shall she come in? were 't good?
> I think she stirs again. No. What's best to do?
> If she come in, she'll sure speak to my wife—
> My wife! my wife! what wife? I have no wife.
> O insupportable! O heavy hour!
> Methinks it should be now a huge eclipse
> Of sun and moon, and that th' affrighted globe
> <Did> yawn at alteration.

It is Othello's world that yaws (" yawns "); shaken, too, with
horror at the vanity in his own " methinks ". The earth holds
on its way and Othello grips the stanchion of his valiantness,
shaken at himself:

> I am not valiant neither,
> But every puny whipster gets my sword.
> But why should honour outlive honesty?
> Let it go all.

Othello awakens from the nightmare to find remorse implicit
in all his proceedings. He does not just now discover Desdemona's chastity: there was no mistake. The love he made
undid him. He knows with all too certain clarity where he has
arrived; it is where he has all the time been heading:

> Here is my journey's end, here is my butt
> And very sea-mark of my utmost sail.

He places himself, in effect, with the tragic lovers in the
second circle of Dante's Hell, for it is remorse and defeat he
feels, not utter shame:

> O cursed, cursed slave! Whip me, ye devils,
> From the possession of this heavenly sight!
> Blow me about in winds! roast me in sulphur!

> Wash me in steep-down gulfs of liquid fire!
> O Desdemon! dead Desdemon! dead! O! O!

The torments are physical and of his own choosing. Torments
are what he can better understand—

> An honourable murderer, if you will;
> For nought did I in hate, but all in honour

—better than the obscure satisfaction of the destruction, the
ineluctable need served by murderous jealousy. Yet:

> Then must you speak
> Of one that loved not wisely but too well

is true too, despite that Othello, going out on his dignity,
still inclines to view himself as in the right, as much as to say
still, " I'd see her dead first."

CHAPTER IV
Unholy Cords

The subject of Othello's agony is a person "so lovely fair" and who "smell[s] so sweet / That the sense aches at [her]"; but the Macbeths become "too intrinse t'unloose", most marvellously devoted, in pursuit of an intangible, their imagination of the crown. Mysteriously, "the golden round" draws them to commit regicide, murder the innocent and draw upon themselves certain retribution by grasping rule as they throw down its foundation in allegiance.* The throne draws Macbeth with an attraction which the trappings of power hardly begins to explain. Rather the absence from his intentions of all forethought of their likely outcome is precisely what leaves thrilling, undetermined possibility predominant. His thoughts waver towards what it might actually mean to kill the King and he is overcome by a vision of pity invincibly "striding the blast" that prevents him from seeing beyond it. Finding himself up against human kindness he only learns the capacity to be up against it. Triumphant personal success in the war, his thoughts bending to unexpressed possibilities, and unlooked-for prognostications all coinciding, he comes to himself there—about to murder the King. When his wife catches his elation and dedicates herself to bring it off for them it is already in a motion of inspiration.

* Cf. "... the Macbeths, almost the only lovingly married couple in Shakespeare, whose love for each other is *the same* as their monstrous creativity in murder. Lady Macbeth is *femme inspiratrice*, and the concentration of Macbeth's love upon her is the only source of inspiration for the artistic slaughter which is what he wants of the world. Macbeth *wants* the bloody horrors of the end of the play, but it takes his love to allow him to realize his ambition." (Ian Robinson, *The Survival of English*, Brynmill Press, p. 198) Whitaker, e.g., thinks Macbeth's desire explicable: "The theme of *Macbeth* is ... the causes and consequences of human sin, of which the story of Macbeth is an *exemplum*. This theme dominates the entire play. Its opening shows temptation at work upon Macbeth, who is a brave and kind man but, like all the fallen sons of Adam, subject to the promptings of appetite—in this case desire for the crown." (Virgil K. Whitaker, *The Mirror up to Nature*, San Marino, Huntington Library, 1965, p. 261)

The inspiration in which Macbeth himself "moves like a ghost," the agent of Murder, to take what his evil intuition holds out to him, comes to him in the form of knowledge, made excitingly sure by Lady Macbeth's proud and quick anticipation of it, of what he can certainly do ("what cannot you and I perform?" she is inspired later to say). The proud mastery of will is the flowering of their marriage. And it fascinates. After Macbeth's inspired conduct in the repulse of the invaders the King comes courting him, and can never sufficiently put over his gratitude to this man who is "so far before": and, until the malady grows so bad that it generates its own cure, Scotland is nonplussed. The suggestion of an inevitable righting of the scales is grounded, however, in an inevitability in the nature of Macbeth's inspiration. If a law is demonstrated, yet there is no suggestion of blind Fortune about the vehicle. Shakespeare's rough-and-ready but effective device for placing Macbeth's desires in an impersonal perspective, the Witches, serves the suggestion of a larger fate. But Blake's assertion that the "weird sisters" are "goddesses of destiny" is extraordinary, in that the sisters are also manifestly witches of the most conventional, "double, double, toil and trouble" conception and have no divine power but only manifest the power of divination. Macbeth listens to them with so manifest a will to be tempted, however, even by such temptresses, as to make Blake's ascription to them of power over destiny right. The destiny, though—Shakespeare's dubious Parcae makes the point—is in Macbeth, impersonal as the law it demonstrates may nevertheless be. The weird sisters' connection with what he is about irritates Macbeth as much as it gives assurance of the nature of what he is about—they are right all the time about what is going to happen to him: and in this respect the First Folio spelling "wayward" for "weird", adding the play on words to the ambiguity in which these beings are invested for Macbeth, brings out their tantalizing indifference and exactly expresses "the force of destiny" as it is exhibited in this play. It is not only from Aristotelian decorum that Shakespeare does not populate his Scottish moor with Eumenides or other such classical furies as he might have found in, say, Ovid:

The furious fiende *Tisiphone* doth cloth hir out of hand
In garment streaming gorie bloud, and taketh in hir hand
A burning Cresset steept in bloud, and girdeth hir about
With wreathed Snakes, and so goes forth. And at hir
> going out,
Feare, terror, grief and pensiveness for companie she tooke,
And also madnesse with his flaight, and gastly staring looke:

(Ovid, Metamorphoses, transl. Golding, IV. 595–600)

but only with contemporary witches. The Witches are not so
suspiciously supernatural as to make Banquo keep an effect-
ively vigilant eye on Macbeth: they nevertheless allure Macbeth. They make his lust palpable to his mind, with the
result that his natural repugnance to murder and horror of
being a murderer more than anything else stimulates him
(being undeniable horror) to the conviction that here is something real. His horror at least being beyond doubt shows him
that whatever he may be about, whatever relation that may
bear to probability, it is not dreaming. This stimulated conviction is the form the promise to Lady Macbeth and him
takes and through it Lady Macbeth finds Macbeth, more
deeply than ever before, with deep faith to chastise him with
the valour of her tongue so that they should not fail. The
unlooked-for warrant of the " wayward sisters " generates an
élan upon which Macbeth's life gathers to a climax, the passion
for which stops him from being judicious (with respect to the
Witches, even ordinarily percipient) even when he is brought
to enunciate with the last certitude that " we still have judgement here." His saying it means only that he has done with
its consideration, and he immediately stands dream-struck
with elation at the pity and terror of what he is to do.
 " Moving like a ghost " recoiled in abstraction from the
horror that he courts, Macbeth proves that for all his conscience's clear imperative (he is never morally deluded) it
can be manipulated, and if not inhibited then better, put to
use. The exultant delusion to which he succumbs is that he
can manipulate human nature—his own. It all falls apart

when expedient evil breeds necessary evil and foul deeds have
to be done, not to defeat the tedious present but by any means
to patch up safety. Then, bound to suffer the circumstances
of his creation, he swells in ignorant self-sovereignty which
only deludes him further until he has no freedom but responds
automatically to the contingencies that arise, and his great
promise lets him down into a drear subjection. Macbeth
seizes free will with resolution, only to destroy himself and
be left knowing nothing but that his will does not belong to
him. Yet he cannot but take hold of the glory so held out
to him.*

The Witches are set apart in the play by the conventionality
of the blasted heaths, mists, cauldrons and spells with which
they are associated. Their connection with human passions
consequently shocks. It suggests that the passions to which
they are attached might in some sense be merely as pheno-
menal as they, who wreck and destroy because it is their
nature. Men repelling an invasion of their homeland are for
them at a " hurlyburly " which will be " lost and won ": they
have their prey singled out in advance of that. They wait on
a human destiny, to foster it in its natural growth, its owner's
identity being no concern of theirs.

Its owner's exploits are reported to the King by a " bleeding
Captain " who does not stop to expunge the horrors of war

---

* The inability, though, has nothing to do with what Manlove calls a
"lack" in Macbeth : "The evidence is that in this play Shakespeare's main
interest is less in Macbeth's positive motive—whatever that may be—for
killing the king, than in the absence in him of a motive for not doing so.
He is concerned with the fact that though Macbeth sees many reasons which
would stay his hand, he still goes on; and he is concerned with the nature
of those reasons, and what they reveal about him. . . . Thus Macbeth is
shown as coming to the murder of Duncan more out of a lack in himself than
out of any particular motive. Unlike Banquo, he did not have in him the
capacity to resist the idea of killing the king." (Colin N. Manlove, *The Gap
in Shakespeare*, London, Vision Press, 1981, p. 145)   Robinson's view of
Macbeth's " passionate desire " is surely more convincing : " Macbeth's crime
is, more or less, unmotivated; he conceives a passionate desire to be king—
and to be a bloodthirsty tyrant—and fatally indulges these passions; his
struggle is to indulge them, with the help of his wife. . . . Macbeth's
struggles are towards the senseless savagery of the end of the play. That
career is not merely the right consequence of his action, it is what he *wants*.
He fulfils his nature."—Ian Robinson, " The Witches and Macbeth ", *The
Critical Review*, Melbourne, xi, 1968, pp. 103-4

from his words but offers their savour, so that the King's approval of what he is told sounds a touch enthusiastic:

> he unseamed him from the nave to th' chops,
> And fixed his head upon our battlements.

Duncan. O, valiant cousin! worthy gentleman!

Duncan smiles, nods, and lets the battle-weary officer tell it: " Mark, king of Scotland, mark!" The despatches have in them all the dread of rebellion, invasion and flaunting challenge instilling fear by " terrible numbers ", and Duncan's gratitude sounds inadequate to the fear and courage they bespeak. His part is only to ratify the victory: " Great happiness! ... What he hath lost, noble Macbeth hath won." But Macbeth musingly finds himself, when the " instruments of darkness " close with him, the vanquisher, by determined courage and a famous personal assault, of a contender for the throne.

The " wayward sisters ", agents of such misfortunes as livestock epidemics, insanity and shipwreck, " the Weird Sisters, hand in hand, / Posters of the sea and land ", cast dispassionate, workers' eyes over their material and watch as their next job comes musing over the heath casting the day's profit and loss. His destiny speaks to Macbeth in their riddles that startle him with their correspondence to close and inadmissible desires of his own, and in their prediction of success in what he hardly yet dare own to be his ambition. The Witches' tempting mysteriousness making evil palpable, they do not deceive Macbeth but rather stimulate him to deceive himself, disabling in him any sense of what is probable by placing before him what in itself is elatingly possible. His startled attention to the " sisters " shows desire for the glory they promise him to be latent in his breast as they materialize before him: it shows him to be on course to murder the King. In respect of their unsought intervention he is " Wrecked as homeward he did come " like the pilot over whose misadventure they gloat: the misfortune of meeting them is a hazard of Macbeth's calling, too. It is not the Witches, but Macbeth who is mysterious. Like the assassination, a normal occurrence in world affairs then as now, the Witches are sensational and the usual thing. But Macbeth is coming to commit an assassination, and he pays them profound heed. It is with a fearful satisfaction that he encompasses the enormity of the crime and the guilt that, better than anyone, he knows attaches itself to murder. A clear, frightening sight of evil only has the effect of making him sure, and hopes such as that " here, / But here, upon this bank and shoal of time, / We'ld jump the life to come ", whose vanity and attraction alarm him, fill him with conviction. For to go " beyond the use of nature" becomes precisely his desire: as his doubts pull they make him feel he holds the reins.

He wonders " So foul and fair a day I have not seen " and the Witches are there. Macbeth is curious—" Speak, if you can: what are you?": it is Banquo who describes them to himself and decides that though they "look not like th'inhabitants o'th'earth, / And yet are on't," they must be witches, who can divine the future: " If you can look into the seeds of time, / And say which grain will grow and which will not [quoting Scripture at them], / Speak then to me ...." Assuming that that's the style, he is jocular about them with Macbeth: " Good sir, why do you start, and seem to fear / Things that do sound so fair?" Macbeth does not join him in this but is amazed and openly interested:

> Say from whence
> You owe this strange intelligence, or why
> Upon this blasted heath you stop our way
> With such prophetic greeting. Speak, I charge you.

The thoughtful ride away from the battle's fruitful expense of violence, the lonely place, and the secrets of his mind suddenly started thus, combine to materialize for him a crisis—he starts, to figure his situation by the emblematic exclamation, " Upon this blasted heath you stop our way." An unrealized direction is made actual. The uncanniness of the Witches is for Macbeth alone until Banquo catches in his companion's voice the vibration of expectant belief, and reads it in his face: Macbeth hears their riddling declarations as clear as bells. To feel for his ground he replies to Banquo's banter, to sound him; Banquo upon this retreats into solemnity:

> But 't is strange:
> And oftentimes, to win us to our harm,
> The instruments of darkness tell us truths,
> Win us with honest trifles, to betray 's
> In deepest consequence.

Banquo's acquaintance with instruments of darkness evidently amounts to a commonplace of information. It is Macbeth who unsettles him, putting him on the protesting defensive before he can have any real inkling of the other's interest. In Banquo's instinctive shying here Macbeth receives his first intimation of the security that lies in the very enormity of his project; in his being " so far before " that where he is is not to be guessed.

When he can examine his mind Macbeth finds that he is horror-struck and exulted. The way ahead lies plain, to the " swelling act / Of the imperial theme " and the mortal glory of a creative imagination that believes only in what is to come. The Witches' mocking assertions make the glory irresistible, attracting purely as they repel. Macbeth feels " the future in the instant " without his wife's prompting to it—the difficulty for him is never how to overcome the desire not to be led into temptation, but only how to fulfil his " black and deep desires ", which thus become, in the attraction of their horror, temptation. He uncovers his soul to his desires unaffectedly; and they are stimulated by a fear that, though involuntary, works to fix his will and shut out conscience:

> If good, why do I yield to that suggestion
> Whose horrid image doth unfix my hair,
> And make my seated heart knock at my ribs,
> Against the use of nature?

He goggles at the " horrid image " until nothing is real but it —and the fact that he asks himself why he so yields denies the candour of " yield ". Why indeed? The " horrid image " incites him to the attention he pays it, his revulsion from it stimulates his desire, and his " horrible imaginings " only prove his " black and deep desires ":

> Present fears
> Are less than horrible imaginings:
> My thought, whose murder yet is but fantastical,
> Shakes so my single state of man that function
> Is smothered in surmise, and nothing is
> But what is not.

As he addresses himself to his imaginings, naming their content, the desire in his words overcomes their thought as his surmise smothers his function. The reality of his " single " or solitary state becomes, as he gives utterance to his state, the reality of what he is to bring to be. The last elliptical phrase figures his being wound up to a standstill, suspended vacant before his future, whose necessity only can fulfil him, the necessity behind " horrible imaginings ". Is the " what is not " that is all there is just murder? And why should that, then, be so much more to him than something he might do? About murder he may hedge, in fact, with " chance may crown me "; but still the more he tastes horror the more he is nothing if not a murderer. His conscience shrinks before " nature ", and he carries on by savouring that sensation of recoil, and telling himself what it is like. Unlike his wife in her triumphant pounce of masterdom, he temporizes with " time and the hour ", and is always anxious to reach Banquo's mind, needing to gather some sense of himself thus if only to be reassured of how far gone he is; yet the vital commitment in all of it is to bring to be the transcending reality. Lady Macbeth seizes with alacrity her chance to complete him as an instrument, and makes herself perfect in her will, as she knows he cannot be. Her wilful denial of her humanity is her admiring tribute to him and to what he is coping with on their behalf.

Cawdor's rebellion is an attempt at a standard *coup d' état*. When it fails, Duncan grieves for him; Cawdor asks to be forgiven and accepts his sentence. Macbeth's attempt has its category in political history too, only in the play the contrast is between a fight and this: Macbeth, the newly-ennobled patriot, plans to receive the King in his own home and stab him to death in his bed, then to blame the servants. Duncan cannot know how he is understood when he greets Macbeth with " The sin of my ingratitude even now / Was heavy on me. Thou art so far before ... ." He cannot read in Macbeth's reply any sensibility of his being out in front where his success as a war-lord places him; and Macbeth does not say the following without apprehension; but when he does say it he learns a capacity:

> The service and the loyalty I owe,
> In doing it pays itself. Your highness' part
> Is to receive our duties ... .

Nemesis overhauls that audacity when, exercizing the same assurance, but after his own deeds have taught men to read him, Macbeth publicly regrets Banquo's absence from the feast to which he is bidden and his ghost comes instead. There, it is an hysterical attempt at urbanity ("Here had we now our country's honour roofed ..."), but here it is a certitude—boosted by his sovereign achievement in action—that his naure can take its due and not pay. Seeing where the King is most vulnerable (in his trust) Macbeth interprets this by acting as though a king's connection with his throne were arbitrary, and regal power homogeneous and transferable.

Macbeth is not cunning, as his subsequent decline into bullying shows, but his "determined wickedness" (in a phrase of Dr Johnson's*) is compelled out of him. The boost that his ability just to pronounce his intentions gives him shows his deep need to mean them; shows the depth from which his desire springs:

> Stars, hide your fires!
> Let not light see my black and deep desires:
> The eye wink at the hand; yet let that be,
> Which the eye fears, when it is done, to see.

As he embraces fear, gets into effectual connection with it, his sapient passion falls deliberating; and, thinking to further his " black and deep desires ", Macbeth is more subject to them than he can know.

* *Johnson on Shakespeare*, ed. Walter Raleigh, Oxford University Press, 1925, p. 171

Macbeth "burns" with "desire" for mortal glory, greatness, of which the crown is the tangible symbol and crimes
the convincing assurance. His letter to his wife is full of
belief in himself and in them both:

> ... they have more in them than mortal knowledge.
> When I burned in desire to question them further, they
> made themselves air, into which they vanished. Whiles
> I stood rapt in the wonder of it, came missives from
> the king, who all-hailed me, 'Thane of Cawdor', by
> which title, before, those Weird Sisters saluted me, and
> referred me to the coming on of time, with 'Hail, king
> that shalt be!' This have I thought good to deliver thee
> (my dearest partner of greatness) that thou mightst not
> lose the dues of rejoicing, by being ignorant of what
> greatness is promised thee. Lay it to thy heart, and fare-
> well.

The dread belonging to this great affair of his manhood does
not get into the letter which is to convey the gift of Fortune
to his wife and to boast of it ("by being ignorant of what
greatness is promised thee"), hence to stir up their pride by
mutual gloating. "Chance may crown me" and palpitations
are merely private and do not touch the sublimity of their
affair. Lady Macbeth dedicates herself to the vaunting pride
he shows her in the joyous note, and immediately proclaims
the fiat:

> Glamis thou art, and Cawdor, and shalt be
> What thou art promised.

Her resolution is not from doubt of him but on the contrary,
from belief in his resolution: she battens on to it, inspired by
belief in what they can do together. Othello and Desdemona
knew no such fulfilment in each other as Lord and Lady Macbeth in their great undertaking, or Desdemona anything of
Lady Macbeth's desirous assumption to herself of her husband's inspiration:

> Hie thee hither,

> That I may pour my spirits in thine ear,
> And chastise with the valour of my tongue
> All that impedes thee from the golden round,
> Which fate and metaphysical aid doth seem
> To have thee crowned withal.

Lady Macbeth is not "subdued" to her husband as Desdemona would be but lusts to know and make real the object of his desire. Her love is not a contentment but a living belief. As Macbeth overcomes dread she dares hell, in the most terrible terms her passionate nature can conceive, to take her womanhood and close her to pity, so that she shall not fail her husband from flaws in her will:

> Come, you spirits
> That tend on mortal thoughts, unsex me here,
> And fill me, from the crown to the toe, top-full
> Of direst cruelty! Make thick my blood,
> Stop up th' access and passage to remorse,
> That no compunctious visitings of nature
> Shake my fell purpose, nor keep peace between
> Th' effect and it!

If Macbeth lets fear work him ("yet let that be / Which the eye fears, when it is done, to see"), yet Lady Macbeth's devotion to evil is a product of his fearful certitude. She does not know Macbeth's equivocal compulsion, or the trouble that his greater scope in the world brings, but can defy murder, giving herself to evil, and the enormity is a defiance, a daring of the depths into which she intends that her arrogance should carry her.

Macbeth, closing with reality as reality becomes the deed, or nothing at all, must cope with more than just "compunctious visitings of nature", and cannot so adroitly decide to have done with "human kindness" as she. Lady Macbeth is more reckless than he, and wrests opportunity where he commits himself to a current of horror that sweeps him away; nevertheless what Dr Johnson calls her sophistries come from as genuine an intention as his "let that be ... ":

> Come to my woman's breasts
> And take my milk for gall, you murd'ring ministers,
> Wherever in your sightless substances
> You wait on nature's mischief! Come, thick night,
> And pall thee in the dunnest smoke of hell,
> That my keen knife see not the wound it makes,
> Nor heaven peep through the blanket of the dark,
> To cry 'Hold, hold!'

Yet again, for all the sincere cruelty of her insistence on the keen knife and the wound and seduction of the worst guilt imaginable (to jilt it when it comes in earnest) her passionate determination is not terrible as the grasp of Macbeth's fear is. His "why do I yield?" is a yielding, as frightened as it is a dishonest question; but Lady Macbeth does not yield to horror but pre-empts it, striving to match him.

Thus the crown and its glory become the way of Macbeth's faith as man and husband; the splendour of that is the cause of Lady Macbeth's unalloyed rapture:

> Great Glamis! worthy Cawdor!
> Greater than both, by the all-hail hereafter!
> Thy letters have transported me beyond
> This ignorant present, and I feel now
> The future in the instant.

She is transported by the certitude brought by the depth of evil they are plumbing, hence her transport has a face of arrogance: " this ignorant present " she says in reckless elation, and that later appears as murderous contempt of the King's servants, " who must bear the guilt / Of our great quell." In her belief everything is possible, which is, finally, as fatal a conviction as Macbeth's erection of evil before his shying mind. Enraptured, both are lost: Lady Macbeth's exulting " unsex me here " (impious hope!) she simply disdains to see as would-be. What Dr Johnson calls in her speech here (he mistakenly says Macbeth's) " the utmost extravagance of determined wickedness " indicates the overbearing elation. What is real is the desire behind it. Johnson's contemptuous

animadversions on her unelevated diction, her " risible "
image of " the blanket of the dark ", the baseness of terms
like *knife*, show indeed with what purposeful scorn Lady
Macbeth addresses herself to subduing her sense of the mean
nastiness of the murder. Heaven peeping through the blanket
is a deliberately mean, sensation-mongering image of the deed.
The keen knife is as vicious as murder, and as mean. Scornful
alike of blood and apprehension, she succeeds by sensation-
alism in getting the evil for the moment out of her heart and
into her head, where she is confident she can deal with it.
She dwells intuitively on her husband's affair of the stabbing
so as to bring herself to the pitch of cruelty requisite for what
he and she have to do.

It is a perfect accord that unites them—and that betrays her
into the enormous sophistry which, the enormity measuring
the belief, gives her belief the form of arrogant self-deception.
Passionately at one with him, her wilfully disregarded falseness comes out in euphemisms for murder and a peculiar
naïveté of expectation:

> He that's coming
> Must be provided for: and you shall put
> This night's great business into my despatch,
> Which shall to all our nights and days to come
> Give solely sovereign sway and masterdom.

What Lady Macbeth wants is unperplexing to her soul. (Yet
when the opportunity lovingly to serve her lord presents itself
she says, " Had he not resembled / My father as he slept, I had
done 't.") She can disown her nature with " I have given
suck ... " but only in deep response to Macbeth's elation, and
in the end the grip and attention summoned to the endeavour
is merely false, an impassioned delusion. Lady Macbeth is
made capable of deciding in the face of all human probability
(to look at it only from the standpoint of likelihood) that they
can achieve " solely sovereign sway and masterdom " for all
their future days and nights (she does not have in mind only
the executive sway) by treasonous murder—her imagination
soars to the transcendence of success and, where it connects
her with her husband, stops there.

It is as the King and Banquo pause before the Macbeths'
castle to smell the hill air and exchange civilities, observing the
birds nesting trustingly on the walls, that what is within the
walls shows finally as evil without reservation. In the presence
of Lord and Lady Macbeth we are carried along by the urgency
of masterful passion. But in the perspective of Banquo's com-
mendation of " This guest of summer, / The temple-haunting
martlet ", and " the heaven's breath " which " smells woo-
ingly here," Lady Macbeth's confidently wicked injunction
to Macbeth to " look like th'innocent flower, / But be the
serpent under't " shows fully its gloating depravity. Duncan,
ever eager to praise Macbeth, compliments Lady Macbeth on
her husband's " great love ", and the gallantry, caught too in
Banquo's appreciative tone, shows the real nature of that love
to be unimaginable. Something makes Banquo guarded with
Macbeth, but he has no inkling of what—nor could he, until
the deed itself should have closed the divide between them.

Macbeth himself, looking into the dazzling future of all his
days, is unable to make the leap in advance of action, and
his wife instinctively disregards it. She overwhelms all consideration: and he does not decide either, but dallies with his
judgement and lets the current of desire bear him along:

> If it were done when 'tis done, then 'twere well
> It were done quickly: if th' assassination
> Could trammel up the consequence, and catch
> With his surcease, success; that but this blow
> Might be the be-all and the end-all ... here,
> But here, upon this bank and shoal of time,
> We 'ld jump the life to come.

He then squanders humane agonizings, rocking between
honest repugnance and considerations of expedience, until the
objection to murder is worn down to its setting a dangerous
example to his subjects (" we but teach / Bloody instructions,
which being taught return / To plague th'inventor "), and
our still having " judgement here " to whether he is prepared
to take the rough with the smooth. Allegiance and hospitality,
" strong both against the deed " indeed! become, when ang-

uished over, at the mercy of his considerations, which then are to be weighed with what courage and adventurous aspiration demand. Consideration damns Macbeth, making arguments of the tenets of humanity, such as that

> his virtues
> Will plead like angels, trumpet-tongued, against
> The deep damnation of his taking-off.

His very repugnance he makes serve his will. When Macbeth suffers a vision of pity, a naked baby inviolate before blasts of rude force, tenderness invincible in the human breast, it is only as a lamentation of hopelessness, a groan of acquiescence in the inevitable:

> And pity, like a naked new-born babe,
> Striding the blast, or Heaven's cherubin, horsed
> Upon the sightless couriers of the air,
> Shall blow the horrid deed in every eye,
> That tears shall drown the wind.

But the deep imaginative possession of the reality he is to bring to be, of every man's hand being turned against him, of the impossible vanity of his usurpation of conscience and his opposing human nature, is in effect—for first of all Macbeth has a discouraging vision, then he stabs the King—a drawing back the better to leap.

Lady Macbeth has no need to be Macbeth's Iago, for he is the last man to need an evil demon to tell him things he would hear but fears to think, but she tunes him up with a display of scornful confidence in them both, mocks at him to keep him true, and the devilry is love even where the jibe is " love ":

> From this time
> Such I account thy love. Art thou afeard
> To be the same in thine own act and valour
> As thou art in desire?

Iago untunes Othello, dissociating him from himself, but Lady Macbeth's " When you durst do it, then you were a man " is pure admiration, as sincere in intention as the avowal with which she enforces it is vile: that she would dash out the brains of the baby at her breast if she had sworn to do so as he has sworn to kill the King. The sophism that Johnson called it, its scorn of unmanning considerations strokes Macbeth's pride, so that he protests his manhood—indulged, proud and passionately sincere, the valour of Lady Macbeth's tongue thrills her husband with desire and winds him into tune on the keynote of " we ":

> We fail?
> But screw your courage to the sticking-place,
> And we 'll not fail.

Whereupon they conclude a derisory plot to put the blame for the King's murder on his attendants by placing the bloody knives in their sleeping hands: " Will it not be received ... / That they have done 't?"

> I am settled, and bend up
> Each corporal agent to this terrible feat.

Macbeth's strength lies in compassing the feat, not in any covering of the traces—of course it is never to be " so received " by anyone, but the notion of blaming the grooms is blatantly a form, to inspire themselves with the conviction that they can do anything. Lady Macbeth's proud scorn of fools stimulates her husband's pride in her and in himself as her consort, and he is not taunted or argued, but stroked into murder. Neither deigns to attend to the sense of her scheme, whose sole virtue lies in the scornful finality with which it is announced—let the grooms be the scapegoats, the likelihood is immaterial: " Who dares receive it other?" Lady Macbeth savours arrogant power, and Macbeth's mouth waters. All the same, his resolution is leaden enough: " False face must hide what the false heart doth know."

Banquo, on watch, picks up the moral unbalance, but like the Elsinore sentinels he is ignorant of the nature of his fear. As darkness encourages his thoughts to range, he only prays to retain control of them. Only a prickliness at Macbeth's desire to sound his mind betrays Banquo's trouble. The power to discount human nature stimulates Macbeth the more any idea of so doing visibly eludes Banquo, trying to put his finger on what is wrong; and Macbeth walks in elation.

The visionary dagger bursts through his glory and forces his gaze to rest upon the image of the fact of murder. In fascination he addresses himself to the reality of murder, telling himself what the instrument is and does:

> or art thou but
> A dagger of the mind, a false creation,
> Proceeding from the heat-oppressed brain?
> I see thee yet, in form as palpable
> As this which now I draw.
> Thou marshall'st me the way that I was going,
> And such an instrument I was to use!

His possession of the fact of murder happens to him, shocking his dream of acquiescence to make him know the utter illusion of his self-mastery. When the inevitability of his achieving this fact possesses him, the blood of the actual fact appearing on the " blade and dudgeon " even as he gazes—then he can dispel it: " There's no such thing: / It is the bloody business which informs / Thus to mine eyes." Macbeth can yet regard the murder as hypothetical (" fantastical "), it appears, but the peremptory vision dispels wishful thinking, the dismaying dagger—" and such an instrument I was to use "—objectifying, and forcing him to address himself to, his end. Even as he groans under the imposition he is possessed by a vision of the spirit of murder, and murder possesses him, not as a proposition, but as a frightening picture—of himself : " Withered Murder ... towards his design / Moves like a ghost." Between this and " Tomorrow, and tomorrow, and tomorrow ... " lies only the realization, the unfolding, and the increasing clarification:

> Now o'er the one half-world
> Nature seems dead, and wicked dreams abuse
> The curtained sleep; Witchcraft celebrates
> Pale Hecate's off'rings; and withered Murder,
> Alarumed by his sentinel, the wolf,

> Whose howl's his watch, thus with his stealthy pace,
> With Tarquin's ravishing strides, towards his design
> Moves like a ghost.

He is withered Murder, as he finds the words rise to his lips: he is as inexorable as a ghost: yet he wills this possession, wills to know everything and to follow out the knowledge to its worst conclusion. His tremendous imaginative prospect of evil—of the earth hanging in space, lit over one hemisphere, the other the domain of sleep where "nature seems dead" and evil is loose—is but the image of his own agency. Perceiving the fact of evil with the shock of a recognition of himself, he knows himself elected. The enormity of that figures itself to him as the earth itself crying out against him:

> Thou sure and firm-set earth,
> Hear not my steps, which way they <may> walk,
> > for fear
> The very stones prate of my whereabout,
> And take the present horror from the time,
> Which now suits with it.

Yet he wants this. The guilty apprehension "suits," and his prayer is only that he may hold on to it. His invocation to horror is also an affirmation of service of it and belief in it, and at the point of drifting into murder Macbeth finds himself acting as Murder's celebrant.

Macbeth sees what he is with only too bewildering clarity. Think of the pride in Hamlet's imagination, of Othello's *aplomb* and of the reassurance in Lear's will to pull his world down about him, and paradoxically it is only Antony in his strong bondage to Venus who looks quite so involuntary a sufferer as the deliberate usurper, Macbeth. Macbeth's crime punishes him almost from its conception, for his passion is masterful but the glory it promises always recedes from his grasp. The great desire by which he is possessed has no real object but itself. ("Doing it all for his wife" is a straw at which he clutches when he finds himself out of his depth, and which Lady Macbeth looks at bemused.) They are lost together, and gone to the extent that their behaviour at the commission of the act of desire verges in its dissociation on the macabre comic.

The assassination is manifestly a feat: Lady Macbeth, fortified with alcohol, gives herself a running commentary while Macbeth is "about it" to keep her mind off ambient night-noises, and has to make grim jokes to cope:

> Hark! Peace:
> It was the owl that shrieked, the fatal bellman,
> Which gives the stern'st good-night.

Macbeth's post-action lamentations give her back her self-command but her courage exists only as counterpart of his dismayed determination, and her chorus is for both their benefits: "A foolish thought, to say a sorry sight," "Consider it not so deeply," "What do you mean?" The sincerely "extravagant wickedness" of her disdain for their other victims, the grooms, stiffens Macbeth to accomplish his doom of a false murderer, which will not let him pose in any such a useful attitude, and together they make up an effective instrument. In the event Macbeth reliably performs what Lady Macbeth shrinks from ("had he not resembled / My father as he slept ... ") even though afterwards he says:

> One cried "God bless us!" and "Amen" the other,
> As they had seen me with these hangman's hands:
> List'ning their fear, I could not say "Amen,"
> When they did say "God bless us"

—he stabs them anyway. It is the cause, and he does it even though

> Methought I heard a voice cry "Sleep no more!
> Macbeth doth murder sleep"—the innocent sleep,
> Sleep that knits up the ravelled sleave of care,
> The death of each day's life, sore nature's bath,
> Balm of hurt minds, great Nature's second course,
> Chief nourisher in life's feast ... .

" Laugh, if you can."* What stops these dire regrets, and especially " I had most need of blessing " (Macbeth holding several wet daggers) from being grotesquely funny is the overwhelming sense that Macbeth—with Lady Macbeth—is suffering, all the time, and not just when it is safely too late to do anything about it. The dagger vision is final, and final—the last reality—as it is calamitous, and the regret coming out a ter the event is no mere fear of the consequences but Macbeth beginning now to taste damnation—in order to see what it is like. The regrets are no retraction but another stage in what he is embarked upon. Macbeth pays with his humanity, knowing the price, and his groans are no more than an invitation to his wife to soothe him and admire it. Dismay and a certitude of betrayal by the gods, which hardens into violence, attend him, but only to prove that in this he is really up against things. Lady Macbeth keeps in spirits by attending to his shaken nerves, and strokes him with

> Why, worthy thane,
> You do unbend your noble strength, to think
> So brainsickly of things,

but her admiration, after the fact, begins to sound got up in order to cope, and too bad to be true. The ecstasy of " this ignorant present " begins to evaporate off reality. As terror lets Macbeth down into nervous apprehension and foreboding, Lady Macbeth comes in, bending her strength to the purpose by talking, of ascendant pitch of tension:

> Infirm of purpose!
> Give me the daggers: the sleeping and the dead
> Are but as pictures: 'tis the eye of childhood
> That fears a painted devil. If he do bleed,
> I'll gild the faces of the grooms withal,
> For it must seem their guilt.

The tense sham indifference, as she talks herself into it, lets her take over and keep on much as Hamlet's frenzy and Othello's

---

* Ludwig Wittgenstein, *Remarks on Frazer's "Golden Bough"*, transl. A. C. Miles and Rush Rhees, Brynmill Press, 1979, p. 3e

nastiness do: but Macbeth's indifference to how the world
" dare receive " his deed is not of pride, but of preoccupation;
for Murder has just handed him his certificate of competency.
He hands over to her not out of weakness but because mere
fortitude were insufficient to overcome his wonder at himself:

> How is 't with me, when every noise appals me?
> What hands are here? ha! they pluck out mine eyes!
> Will all great Neptune's ocean wash this blood
> Clean from my hand? No; this my hand will rather
> The multitudinous seas incarnadine,
> Making the green—one red.

Sounds start thoughts, for the hallucination of murder having
given way to the fact, Macbeth finds himself arrived where he
does not yet know himself. "To know my deed, 't were best
not know myself": but that impossibility is a matter for pride,
too. His incontrovertible deed is incontrovertibly of himself.

The Ordinary Working Man who keeps the castle gate
heralds common day with common chit-chat while he lets in
Anxious Solicitude in the gentlemen who come to wake the
King. Hearing their talk of portents, Macbeth is non-
committal to the point of amusement:

Lennox. The obscure bird
> Clamoured the livelong night: some say, the earth
> Was feverish and did shake.
Macbeth. 'T was a rough night.

He is unnerved only by the tone of disbelief in the voices of
those who discover the corpses; equal to anything but Macduff's theatrical clamour and evident need just to make a
noise, do something other than gape, to unite his wits. Their
simple incomprehension, with Malcolm's dreadfully real
bathos, "O, by whom?", dashes Macbeth, his distance from
these clamouring innocents with their solicitude for their feelings making him fumble. Macduff's foolishness in protecting
Lady Macbeth's feminine susceptibilities, where his own mas-
culine ones are obviously routed, is worse than pointed accusation and, taken off his guard, Macbeth's endeavour to fall in

with the general horror only leaves him "lamenting" Duncan with the most negligent dissembling, half careless confession of his real feelings:

> Had I but died an hour before this chance,
> I had lived a blessed time; for from this instant
> There's nothing serious in mortality.

The odd, out-of-phase lamentation alerts his amazed listeners and in his consequent stage-fright Macbeth concocts an artificial rhetoric of astonishment in the manner of Macduff—"his silver skin laced with his golden blood"—the recklessness in which alone is enough to warn the princes to make themselves scarce. Banquo, in saving the situation with an oath in which all can join, seems to prevent Macbeth ("there's nothing serious ...") from breaking into confessed defiance.

Banquo does not forget that the Witches promised him fairer than Macbeth—"may not they be my oracles as well?"—but interest unites with a dawning understanding only to safeguard his curiosity from temptation. What Macbeth understands as a challenge to usurp the throne Banquo understands as "what will be, will be." He is murdered. It takes Macduff's insupportable remorse at his wife's and children's slaughter, the most dismal of Macbeth's works, to oppose Macbeth. Macduff exposes his family to danger from patriotic concern; Macbeth makes such concern a betrayal of Macduff's deepest love, and the upshot, drawing confused loyalties to a point against him, is his creation as well. He draws it on himself as he becomes increasingly enslaved by circumstances—for instance, sizing up Banquo, whose mind Coleridge describes justly as *"unpossessed ...* wholly present to the present object,—an unsullied, unscarified mirror!"* as a threat to be removed.

Macbeth, interviewing thugs, falls into his wife's handy arrogance and bullies them with contemptuously unpersuasive arguments, the only object of which is to make them feel

---

* "But O! how truly Shakespearian is the opening of Macbeth's character given in the *unpossessedness* of Banquo's mind, wholly present to the present object, an unsullied, unscarified mirror!"—S. T. Coleridge, *Lectures and Notes on Shakespeare and Other Dramatists*, Routledge, n. d., p. 208

their helplessness. The tyrant rant of " are you men or dogs?"
is " who dares receive it other?" declined from elation into
necessary expediency. For the assassins are not the only slaves
of circumstance. Macbeth mentions Fleance as one whom they
had better murder while they are about it, for as basely as
may be he has to tidy up loose ends.

His pride blinds him to the low necessity. He fails to see
that his wife's mind is running along precisely the same lines
as his own: " Is Banquo gone from court? ... Nought's had,
all's spent, / Where our desire is got without content." He
needs to believe she still depends on his faint-heartedness for
her stimulus to courage, because he has something for her
which is to show her that it is not so—a present. When
actually she is looking for an opening to broach a certain
matter, with wifely tact, he butts in with significant dismay-
fulness:

> We have scorched the snake, not killed it ... .
> But let the frame of things disjoint, both the worlds
>   suffer,
> Ere we will eat our meal in fear, and sleep
> In the affliction of these terrible dreams
> That shake us nightly: better be with the dead,
> Whom we, to gain our peace, have sent to peace,
> Than on the torture of the mind to lie
> In restless ecstasy.

He does not solicit her approval but, like a husband, wants
her to know what he is up against on their behalf (hence
the Laertes-reckless " let ... both the worlds suffer ") and to
include her by giving her his troubled brow to caress. The
heroically negligent " better be with the dead " invites her soft
demur. Catching on, she is as reassuring as he asks and urges
him to " Be bright and jovial among your guests tonight";
her attention to his drift joins in the macabre love-game, and
he hints at his plans for Banquo and his son, arousing her
curiosity with

> So shall I, love, and so I pray be you:
> Let your remembrance apply to Banquo;
> Present him eminence, both with eye and tongue ...

with obvious pleasurable anticipation of the moment when he will produce the corpses. At the mention of the name she remembers that she has something to put to him, but is surprised to be forbidden with an exclamation:

> O, full of scorpions is my mind, dear wife!
> Thou know'st that Banquo and his Fleance lives.
> *Lady Macbeth.* But in them nature's copy's not eterne.
> *Macbeth.* There's comfort yet, they are assailable,
> Then be thou jocund: ere the bat hath flown
> His cloistered flight, ere to black Hecate's summons
> The shard-born beetle with his drowsy hums
> Hath rung night's yawning peal, there shall be done
> A deed of dreadful note.
> *Lady Macbeth.* What's to be done?
> *Macbeth.* Be innocent of the knowledge, dearest chuck,
> Till thou applaud the deed.

"Jocund"! Macbeth's deliberate invocation here of that evil which had unignorably possessed him and, as evil, compelled his soul, is wildly deluded by success. As he confidently summons his powers for his wife's admiration she wonders at him, for the magic is applied just where she was herself summoning determination, like Macbeth bending up each corporal agent to a terrible feat again. This time she is beguiled. Now his arrogance disdains to consider that he is compelled to these ignoble murders by circumstances and merely to make himself secure. Only her entrancement permits his rapture, when she would herself have made the suggestion for which he plumes himself had he not mystified her. He exhibits in this the same kind of inspired will as Lady Macbeth did when she bade the ministers of Murder "unsex" her, and she is caught up by Macbeth's rapture rather than by admiration of the rapidity of his invention. He peers into the gathering dusk, adoring the powers of darkness as he puts himself and his agents

among them, all with serious intention, and the convinced
attentive fervour, and the finality of his resolution to " cancel
and tear to pieces that great bond / Which keeps me pale",
are as fatuous. We pity the man who sees himself, in a hallucination, as " withered Murder ", even though the fault is
his own: we pity the owner of such a fault. But the man who
holds himself up to his wife's admiration in the role (sucess-
fully) is pitiable in an ignobler sense. The finality of his
resolution is unavoidably would-be, no longer the finality in
his determination to " let that be / Which the eye fears, when
it is done, to see ". The reality of Macbeth's inspiration of
greatness is a macabre language of love. Gazing past his
wondering wife with visionary eyes he calls upon evil to serve
him and the inspiration of his desire becomes a technique by
which he deludes himself:

> Light thickens, and the crow
> Makes wing to th' rooky wood:
> Good things of day begin to droop and drowse,
> Whiles night's black agents to their preys do rouse.

When Murder, moving " with Tarquin's ravishing strides ",
possessed him, he exclaimed involuntarily, but he invokes
" night's black agents " in a feat and of necessity, and to im-
press his wife with the capacity, no longer to move hand in
hand with her into the unknown. " Thou marvell'st at my
words "—well, she marvels at something. The boost her
mystification gives him is already a development from their
conjoint arrogance, and, as the real magic that was a property
of their desire becomes an instrument, they begin to lose each
other. It is not long after that Lady Macbeth withdraws from
the uncomfortably brightening limelight. Her husband's inspiration ends in excluding her except as the object upon which
he directs his increasingly vain exultation, and while he grows
desperate she grows resigned to suffer what comes.

Macbeth's hospitality at as unfestive a feast as can well be
imagined is a spectacle of will. He switches from the attentive
host to being man-to-man with hired assassins with an actor's
facility, and his brittle assurance gives a hysterical edge to the

proceedings. When he is told of Fleance's escape his dismay is fatuously disproportionate—as though it made all the difference in the world:

> Then comes my fit again: I had else been perfect;
> Whole as the marble, founded as the rock,
> As broad and general as the casing air:
> But now I am cabinned, cribbed, confined, bound in
> To saucy doubts and fears.

He thinks to clinch his safety in this but what is at issue is the integrity of his mind *vis-à-vis* the unanswerable finality of necessary action: his future hinges for the moment on that of a child whom he had thought casually to " despatch ". So much for " night's black agents ". All reduces to a nonsense, he is at the mercy of chance, and now to complete the rout of his stand on devilry comes Banquo's ghost to occupy Macbeth's seat at table.

" I had else been perfect " really expresses disbelief at being let down by the Devil. Macbeth is left without resource, so that when in grim resolution he tries to pull off the surprise for his wife anyway and publicly regrets Banquo's absence from the feast, the sheer face of it is nearly touching:

> Here had we now our country's honour roofed,
> Were the graced person of our Banquo present;
> Who I may rather challenge for unkindness
> Than pity for mischance!

He is going to have the murder a triumph of his and Lady Macbeth's power to do anything, if he has to set his face and stare the Devil out. Lady Macbeth's dissociation from his will now soon enough appears. Conscience rises through his determination in the shape of the wordless ghost and Macbeth is reduced to mad shouting:

> Thou canst not say I did it : never shake
> Thy gory locks at me.

His wife's taunt is near the quick (too near, for her taste, as she scents the hysteria under the wicked joy of her husband's occasion): "Are you a man?" Her own confidence that they can hold on by their wits to what they have begins to drain from her as that becomes in any sense a question with her. The silent accusation of the Ghost annihilates Macbeth's husbandly pride together with his elation and, at the hour of his first devil's triumph, he is left blustering, blown all ways by ungraspable occurrence:

> Ay, and a bold one, that dare look on that
> Which might appal the devil.
> *Lady Macbeth.*   O proper stuff!
> This is the very painting of your fear:
> This is the air-drawn dagger which, you said,
> Led you to Duncan.

The action again verges on the comic-macabre, as she throws his former boasts at him in exasperation. As his astonished grip closes on emptiness, her attentions harden to impatience and her scorn of fortune to scorn of him, quickly resolved into despair ("Hell is murky"). Murder will out, and begins to do so in Macbeth's disintegration as he loses control over the contingencies of his creation.

The ghost in *Macbeth* does not say anything, but it speaks as Macbeth's imagination's terrific veracity and he stands before it as a man accused, not specifically of anything, for answer is denied him, but merely as false: "Thou hast no speculation in those eyes / Which thou dost glare with!" There is nothing to be said to Banquo, and Macbeth can only shout under the ghost's cold glare to occupy his frozen wits: it has made its point, and goes away, when he is reduced to protesting his manhood. Not only his compact with evil but his physical courage itself is mocked in the wrested boast, "What man dare, I dare," and Macbeth is left wondering. Enlightenment is wearying past hope and washes him up at the furthest shore of humanity, the threshold certainty of his animal courage and ability to kill before he is killed:

> For mine own good
> All causes shall give way: I am in blood
> Stepped in so far that, should I wade no more,
> Returning were as tedious as go o'er:
> Strange things I have in head that will to hand,
> Which must be acted ere they may be scanned.

Things "strange", that is, even to the human usurper he would be. It is a boast, but one in which Macbeth's true genius stands confessed. He must now consciously turn from the glory of his imagination to persevere towards an unimaginable goal, through what presents itself to his imagination as a lake of blood surfeiting and wearying horror itself. "We are yet but young in deed" is a despairing boast.

The agents of misfortune in their boffin-like absorption in their formulae are as indifferent to him as the silent phantom; indifferent as beasts to their fallen prey; they speak only to his need to believe, be it in Banquo's merely human reproach to him, which his ghost declines to make, or the Witches' malign animus, which is not that at all. They are up to "a deed without a name", and Macbeth must not only care what they are up to, but seek them out, get through their cackling madness and command them—by the composition of nature, like Lear commanding the elements—to tell him what is in store for him:

> though the treasure
> Of Nature's germens tumble all together,
> Even till destruction sicken; answer me
> To what I ask you.

Macbeth is himself, as we say, sick—he is weary: but the Witches are not to be bidden of his weariness, not because they are crafty but because they are as indifferent as the weather to the identity of the individual upon whose passions they perform. In the pride of his strength Macbeth pre-empts his humanity and the "wayward sisters" attend him and whether he like it or dislike it warrant all that his passion peremptorily intends. When they told Banquo he would beget kings, Banquo was glad about that: when they told Macbeth he would be king, he killed the King. They tell him he is invincible, and he understands them by resolving to slaughter Lady Macduff and her children.

When that is what Macbeth has to do next, there is only the last circle of despair at the judgement of what he is and what he has made that remains for him to descend into. Macduff's shame (" Sinful Macduff, / They were all struck for thee!") is not to be borne, and the anguish he suffers (" I cannot but remember such things were / That were most precious to me ") rallies his humanity to a bitter anger, mightier at last than Macbeth's residual, drear persistence. At the end Macbeth is as surely a lost soul as Lady Macbeth sleepwalking in murky hell. He has his last hour to " strut and fret ", but the pair are lost to each other; there is no more inspiration in their wickedness, and his comment on hearing the news of her death is that she must have died at some time—" There would have been a time for such a word." It is insignificant that it is now. There is terrible knowledge in his recognition that he and she are damned and dissevered, that that is what they have made, and that he cannot wish better for her than to recognize that his defeat and subjection to the circumstances of his creation is hers too.

The avengers come on in the light of day with drums and colours; their object to restore the sovereign, to depose Macbeth merely its means: " To dew the sovereign flower and drown the weeds ". Macbeth's contempt of attendants and pursuers alike is mere defiance of the inevitable, yet going with it is a relish for the fight, and a spark of spirit, too, is in his amused exchange with the rueful Doctor: " What rhubarb, senna, or what purgative drug, / Would scour these English hence? Hear'st thou of them?" And a gleam of the warrior's fire lights his words, tinged with wistful regrets of past exploits: " We might have met them dareful, beard to beard, / And beat them backward home." But he can no longer look to all that; the cry of women and word of his wife's death turn his face upon the inevitable, and there is left him only to see the event to its conclusion. An unmeaning paltering with his soul fills his mind making nonsense of love, courage and adventurous aspiration: only his native fierceness survives his despair:

> Blow, wind! come, wrack!
> At least we'll die with harness on our back.

The "strong toil" of the gods' "grace" to Macbeth is eventually made present to him there, in the strength of his despair; there in "Tomorrow, and tomorrow, and tomorrow, / Creeps in this petty pace from day to day, / To the last syllable of recorded time"; in the hopeless emptiness following the defeat of his endeavours; in Macbeth's creation.

CHAPTER V

The Need

King Lear's professionalism is marred by animosity when, with military decision, he goes to abdicate in favour of his children. The dispositions are all to be fair and unbiased, and when the King defiantly declares that he is getting old— " while we / Unburdened crawl toward death "—he indicates that he means to be coping seriously with a real eventuality. If what accompanies the brusquely advanced intention seems more likely to hinder it, the tone of the old monarch's court takes off some of the oddity. Gloucester boasts of his " fault " in having begotten a bastard and is somewhat deflated when Kent wishes the " issue " well and lets the fault stand. His self-satisfaction allows Gloucester to patronize his son Edmund and not see that Edmund dangerously hates it. The King betakes himself with arrogance to a self-proposed duty, relinquishes his command with a passionate display of command, and provokingly ignores the contradiction between his intention and his behaviour. He states his " constant will ", only to gad away upon an insult, " which of you shall we say doth love us most? " His behaviour challenges his daughters either publicly to defy him and declare themselves insulted, or contemptuously to go along with his whim. Sarcasm— " Where nature doth with merit challenge "—rises as though of itself within his foreboding intention to " express our darker purpose ". The covert hostility is sudden but not, apparently, odd, for the elder daughters rise unsurprised to outface him with blandishments exactly as hostile.

How it goes with the royal family could not be clearer shown than by the character of Goneril's and Regan's *sang-froid* at this public encounter, with its hot-headed and tragical result. Goneril, Regan and Lear understand each other very well; the girls pronounce the wonderful superlatives they are dared to without bothering to demur—their frozen indifference to him lets not so much as a hint of offence trouble their serene compliance:

Dearer than eyesight, space and liberty;
Beyond what can be valued rich or rare;
No less than life with grace, health, beauty, honour ... .

They calmly defy anyone to giggle. The youngest daughter is
nonplussed by it. Alone excluded from the deadly family
game, she looks on and is distressed for her father and not least
for herself, finding herself placed where her sisters are to
secure her dowry and the rightful prospects of a princess.
Whether she believes her father to be serious and to attend
to the flattery he asks for or not, she feels the vibration between
him and her sisters discount her innocence and shut her out.
Whilst Cordelia withdraws upon her candour in defence,
Regan calmly outdoes Goneril in metallic emptiness. Her untroubled professions—" Only she comes too short, that I profess / Myself an enemy to all other joys "—tell Lear plainly
that she knows him and is not about to be goaded by him.
The icy rebuff leaves it with Lear to call his daughters liars.
To do so would be to confess the appeal in his sudden challenge, to admit that the provocation constitutes asking his
daughters if they will hate him if he is good to them; and to
acknowledge that their response says " Yes ". It is a deadlock,
and impossible; the mutual hostility is invincible; Lear can
no more let go his grip and show himself impassioned than
the elder girls can let go theirs and respond with honest anger,
let alone understanding. Yet Lear's suddenness does constitute
an initiative, and his stubbornness a resolution to proceed with
it. He stands by the terms of his challenge with a determination not to be worsted that leaves him depending on his
younger daughter to acquiesce in his masterdom. When
Cordelia shows that here she will not accommodate herself
to him, he repudiates her with passionate finality.
   Cordelia, upset by the vindictive discharge between her
elders, will not allow herself to be made of no account, and
is thus implicated. Her self-reassuring asides (" aloof from
the entire point ") show her hurt by her fortunes' being made
to depend on this dark, unconfessed game of charades which
she does not understand but dislikes:

> Then poor Cordelia!
> And yet not so, since I am sure my love's
> More ponderous than my tongue.

Lear would implicate her by his confidence that her expressions of love will preponderate over her sisters'; she only contends against the stress of wills holding the family locked in conflict, and is made incapable of saying the few simple words that would demonstrate her father's right to command them from her. They would be too momentous: they would negate her; admit her perforce to the evil-charmed circle; and constitute the surrender of her candour. For her father owes her obligations too, with her suitors in attendance. He does not consider that his challenge to Goneril and Regan to defy him, if it includes Cordelia, places her in the position of being judged with her sisters. In placing the onus on her to go along with or defy his presumption he derogates her with a casualness not to be borne. But his pride and angry frustration that he cannot reach his elder daughters blind him to Cordelia's feelings, and the public slight makes it impossible for her to gratify him with an unconsidered acquiescence. To exempt her would be for him openly to admit his desire to touch Goneril and Regan. So Cordelia must be estranged from his heart, and Kent's good sense publicly renounced ("Reserve thy state"). Lear braces himself hard against the upshot, refusing thus the consolation that ought to lie in Cordelia's opposition to his will of an invincible filial respect, and Kent's selfless service.

Lear's inalterably masterful will makes Cordelia stand up to him in a way which forces him to repudiate her in good earnest and against his will, not in any game of ancient antagonism. She deflates his pride telling him that she loves him "as is right fit" and that wives have duties to husbands as well as daughters to fathers, so that he must alter his purpose and contract his expectations. The breach is inevitable, once Lear has applied the pressure. Cordelia's "tenderness"—"So young, and so untender?"—must in reality be filial respect, only Lear cannot bear less than implicit obedience affirming his passionate, antagonistic command. To settle for mutual love, if he had allowed her "tenderness", would be for him

to make terms with the opprobrium attaching to his parenthood, but Lear will no more confess that Goneril and Regan
are what they are than they will acknowledge him. He would
rather endure the fight. He spurns the love of Cordelia and
Kent with a blind vehemence that comes of a need to protect
his coherent will, and his anger turns to madness and punishes
him.* For his deep pride has always to contend against a
will to enforce, not pity, but recognition that he is hurt and
that his need is righteous. He exaggerates with military intent,
so as to be seen to cope with an undeniable anguish:

> For, by the sacred radiance of the sun,
> The mysteries of Hecate and the night,
> By all the operation of the orbs
> From whom we do exist and cease to be,
> Here I disclaim all my paternal care,
> Propinquity and property of blood ... .

The mighty, disproportionate oath is his defence of his em-
battled majesty. He aims to obliterate the cold disclaiming of
the elder daughters, which nothing can reconcile him to owning. To do so would be to change the savour of antagonism
for the loving care of a Cordelia; to forsake the self-
exacerbated, irritable anger necessary to the maintenance of
the man Kent loves. Lear challenges filial love, seeking not
reassurance, which in Cordelia he shamefully gets, but obedience. He wants the strength-bestowing submission whose
warmth would consign Goneril and Regan in their chilly
refusal to an outer darkness, and give him the fire to make
them see him. He is betrayed to dismay because he wanted
not duty or deference so much as the fight and the victory of
Cordelia's loyalty. He is uncandid, regretting Cordelia in the
past tense ("I loved her most, and thought to set my rest /
On her kind nursery"), but it is the mendacity of passionate
need, comparable with the dishonesty in Macbeth's passion,
his "why do I yield?" which is itself a yielding. So Cordelia

* On, particularly, the notion of Lear's suffering as punishment, see David
Sims, "Scald Rymers", *The Human World*, no. 12, 1973, to which the present
discussion is in general indebted.

wishes he might, of course, but what Lear means and intends by "propinquity" is that Cordelia should secure his "rest" by implicit obedience, saving the face of his majesty; hence the pang of regret, disguised as disappointment in her, and betrayed in his recognition of her "kindness". Lear's refusal of comfort in Cordelia ensures that he is able to stiffen in opposition to Goneril and Regan, and in his proud isolation answer their refusal of his plea by coolly augmenting their portions according to the terms stated, with grim abandon thus throwing his power to them to make them use him after their kind.

His action, prompted by pride and inflexible will as it is, arises as much out of what Goneril and Regan are. Kent's "unmannerly" intervention is as vain an appeal to sense as Cordelia's distressed indignation at his defiant recklessness. Lear's refusal to listen to Kent, who is devoted enough to brave his displeasure, belongs with the banishment of Cordelia which prevents him from being saved by her love from the consequences of his pride. The actions of Cordelia and Kent serve inadvertently to madden and exacerbate Lear, though neither would have him mad. But it is just Lear's nature to suffer and take on the children who hate him. He does not want it any other way; his impugned pride stiffens beyond reach. Kent understands him ("Fare thee well, king; sith thus thou wilt appear ...") and in his disguised service aims always to help him endure his wilful suffering. Cordelia, her banishment pronounced to her suitors with irrevocable finality, turns her angry frustration on her sisters and denounces their opportunism, base flattery and abuse of the old man's credulity. A spark of the family fire shows in her disdain to defend herself; determined not to criticise their father, she releases her frustration in her rebuke of her sisters' "cunning":

> If for I want that glib and oily art
> To speak and purpose not, since what I <will> intend,
> I'll do 't before I speak ... .
> But even for want of that for which I am richer—
> A still-soliciting eye, and such a tongue
> That I am glad I have not, though not to have it

Hath lost me in your liking ... .
Time shall unfold what plighted cunning hides ... .

Powerless to correct the injustice of her usage and her exclusion, her righteous indignation derives from a determined refusal to be like Goneril and Regan and criticise her father. She is impatient with the whole set of them. She will not defend herself against her father, but in effect she opposes her will of respectful love against his will of command. She will neither acquiesce nor argue, but in discharging her frustration speaks precisely as Lear refuses to do from pride: clearly it is not only the rebuke to her sisters that is satisfying. Goneril and Regan are set in a cold refusal which Lear is impotent to affect except by inciting them to the cruelty incipient in their dislike. What in his actions he refuses to own is precisely their cruelty—the stony-heartedness they are quite content he should see in them (especially at his own invitation, and with half the kingdom as a reward). His pride works thus to suffer these flesh of his flesh in their inhumanity, in spite of their will to triumph in disavowal and repudiation; only he has not Cordelia's candour to clarify it.

All is dark and passion-obscured. Lear brings his house down about him merely because he cannot resist, in the event, putting a sting in the tail of his good intentions. He wants his watchful children to remain sensible of his authority, no matter what else he relinquishes. And they respond with keen intuition; the women lie not in craft, as Cordelia supposes, but from real dislike, answering the arrogance of their father's insult with a contempt of the plea contained in it which he will not mistake. Goneril says this gloomily meaning it, although it is spoken with malice as well: " The best and soundest of his time hath been but rash; then must we look from his age to receive, not alone the imperfections of long-engraffed condition, but therewithal the unruly waywardness that infirm and choleric years bring with them." The animosity in her pessimism betrays a " long-engraffed condition " itself. This is apparent in the unspoken accord of the two elder sisters on this occasion, which sets the rest of the court in complete disarray and exposes such vulnerability in Gloucester as to incite

Edmund to villainy. As far as intention goes, the mutual and hostile judgement of Lear is not false; it is not affected to mask wickedness with a reasonable face (although that is how it is used). Rather it is sincere, with the dreadful sincerity of Lear's daughters, dehumanized in set repudiation and dislike. Whatever is said and meant, however, Lear has given his daughters scope to flourish according to their breeding. " If our father carry authority with such disposition as he bears, this last surrender of his will but offend us," recognizes Goneril.

Lear's temperament makes intelligible both Goneril's and Regan's unfilial contempt and Cordelia's refusal to acquiesce in his harmful whim. These very different natures are revealed in the situation created by Lear's overweening pride. What is apparent in the contrast between Lear's public appearance of satisfaction with Goneril and Regan (a satisfaction of no duration) and his dismayed rage with those upon whom his authority depends is the degree of wilfulness in his behaviour: he is determined in his turn to outface his daughters, only the energetic, obscure movement of Lear's nature to bring things to a crisis differs from their (perhaps equally dark) resistance of the unconscious aim.

The relations obtaining in Gloucester's family, which seem by contrast indifferent and casual, bear sufficient resemblance to reinforce our sense of what an inevitable, implacable opposition like that between Lear and his elder daughters must store up between them. Gloucester has no deep-rooted preference for either son. His airy proprietorship of Edmund, which Edmund feels as a " tyranny " licensing an equally airy opportunism, is not essentially different from the regard he professes for his " proper " son. Confronted by the story of Edgar's " treachery ", there is nothing of robust sufficiency in either Gloucester or his relations with his son to encourage disbelief or protest: he simply and immediately believes it, and is offended. Gloucester's human relations are characterized by slackness rather than unbelief, and he is lost when his complacent assumptions are shattered. Whilst the story of the awakening of his native courage and loyalty counterpoints that of Lear's strivings, what shines through Gloucester's vices is an essentially simple nature, instinctively mocked by Edmund's stage-villain's delight in setting fools to undo themselves (and it is very nearly the death of him as it inspires Edgar's remedial measures on his behalf). With his self-satisfied stories, surprised, head-scratching mutterings about the way of the world, eagerness to scan portents and to believe in improbable explanations of anything untoward, Gloucester brings Edmund's practices down on him. But he does this in ignorance, and indirection is soon enough resolved when his native decency is given the scope offered by service of Lear and works against habit. Lear has both a much stronger sense of what he is up against and an urgent will to bring it to pass. He moves inexorably and with his eyes open towards disaster, to " make things change, or cease ", as it is said of him; and he is not to be saved from the worst he can bring on himself. Edmund's contemptuously unsubtle play with the fake letter succeeds because Gloucester is noticeably unsettled by the events at court, and so would " unstate [himself] to be in a due resolution ". He clutches at the notion of Edgar's treachery with an urgent need to keep his feet at whatsoever cost. In Edmund's case, his uncaring cruelty is made intelligible by his father's unbelief, for the human disconnection (" His breeding, sir, hath been at my charge ") deprives both sons of the obligations owed to a father. Edgar is left lost and confusedly defensive; Edmund strikes the attitude of one disabused of sentiment (as well the son of such a father might). The amused confidence with which Edmund composes a letter which he knows will deceive his father shows how the King's frustration with his children triggers a loose vitality in the same direction of " son against father ... father against child ". The spirit of antagonism propagated at that centre is sympathetically absorbed by Edmund, filling him with a conviction of moral independence. As Gloucester believes in a moment in Edgar's " treachery ", so Edgar himself is only surprised to hear of it; he is not devastated and astonished, but moves with passive resignation to his own defence. Edmund works as Iago does, to undermine what is already insufficient.

Neither Lear not Goneril seeks to ease or avert the inevitable friction when, under the terms of the abdication settlement, he is quartered on her with a hunting retinue. Instead she cultivates an overbearing, hectoring manner, suggesting constant irritation so as to remain aloof and impenetrable to her father's provocation. But at the same time she is genuinely nettled—not so much by the hundred knights and squires but by Lear's intention to make of them the issue which will break her cold repudiation of him. Lear's train may well constitute a real annoyance, but it is Lear's refusal to lie down, his determination to antagonize and thus to challenge her resolve, that Goneril hates and will not have. His very power to arouse her to hatred she hates. She complains with the exaggeration not of craft, to make an issue, but of real, spiteful annoyance at finding herself not deferred to as absolute mistress in her own home. Her pleasure in the coveted patrimony is quite marred:

> By day and night he wrongs me. Every hour
> He flashes into one gross crime or other
> That sets us all at odds. I 'll not endure it ... .

The vague yet immoderate exaggeration (" flashes into one gross crime or other ") combined with her inflamed and righteous irritability (" sets us all at odds ") shows her determined to stand in opposition. She combats her shame (how unlike Lear's!) that her father with his intractable presence exacerbating the accommodation issue, has the " power to shake [her] *woman*hood thus ". Yet he forces her to maintain the tactic of refusing to acknowledge that he has anything to ask of her, with the result of making her genuinely angry. In spite of her will to disclaim him she exposes herself—exposes her pleasure in countering him at every turn, and in having him the object of her contemptuous reproof. There is nothing but contempt and irritated nerves in the abuse he provokes; she is declared, her incipient cruelty is revealed:

> idle old man,
> That still would manage those authorities
> That he hath given away! Now, by my life,
> Old fools are babes again, and must be used

With checks as flatteries, when they are seen abused.

The savour of the power to hurt him, which he makes her taste by maintaining the situation and being himself, betrays the cruelty in the coldness she maintains:

Goneril.   I'd have it come to question ...
                    ...Prepare for dinner ...
Lear. Let me not stay a jot for dinner; go get it ready.

The conflict of wills is rooted below the level of the inevitable clash over arrangements. The implacable mutual resistance of father and daughter resolves into open conflict as Lear carries off his majesty—hunting, giving orders (he strikes one of Goneril's gentleman-attendants), and roaring in his old voice in the manner Goneril cannot abide. Immoveable in her refusal to listen to him or look on the man he always holds before her in other than contempt, she quivers in a self-perpetuating, repressed fury in which she knows the pleasure of hurting. Lear's headstrong will is not admirable, but the impossibilty that he should go back on what he finds himself set forth upon, the seriousness of the issue to his pride, is shown by the disproportionate opposition it provokes. Will, egotism it may be, but it has warrant in the agony it brings on him and in what his daughters show themselves to be. There is a blind courage in his peremptoriness which, although it does not redeem him as a father, shows at least that what Kent and Cordelia want for him would be impossible. Lear of course always protests, what he believes, that he is only asking to be treated like a father. Goneril as steadily affirms what she is resolved to stand upon even in her own eyes, that she is only talking sense.

    Cordelia, stung by her usage to fly out at her sisters with " I know you what you are," her eyes " washed " with tears of frustration and incomprehension, is yet less than devastated by leaving her father to the deserts of his wilfulness, and departs in anger. Kent's devotion beyond his duty, which urges him to risk all in his lord's service, is different from the filial respect which, as Cordelia says, must not command her to the exclusion of all other affection. Lear's affront to her debases his

fatherhood; his harsh rebuff to Kent offends against a reciprocal duty, for he owes it to Kent to command and receive his
services and to be worth the loyalty he commands. Cordelia
he owes respectful recognition and the guiding attention that
is the love of a parent.

By conspicuously proferring the service that Lear, hard-
beset, had rebuffed, Kent signals his support through the
King's defences:

> Dost thou know me, fellow?
> *Kent.* No, sir; but you have that in your countenance which
> I would fain call master.
> *Lear.* What's that?
> *Kent.* Authority.

The odd challenge in his tone surprises Lear out of his studied
blustering. It reminds him of the feel of majesty, which in
his belligerent defence of it he had begun to forget, and ratifies
the urgent need it serves.

Reassured, Lear keeps to his course, roaring like the King
to outface negligence: "What says the fellow there? Call the
clotpoll back! Where's my fool? Ho! I think the world's
asleep. How now! Where's that mongrel?" The seriousness
of Lear's gusto and belligerence, the counterpart in him of
Goneril's wilful irritation of her nerves to maintain opposition,
appears in his alertness at Kent's reminder, and in his hankering after the Fool, who tells him the truths he cannot for very
self-defence pause to worry out. The Fool's wistful mockery
of the world's voice of reasonableness and common sense and
Kent's dogged solicitude between them prevent his isolation
from leading to despair. They keep alive in him some sense
of where and what he is when his necessary pugnacity obscures
that. Pugnacity confounds equable intention (or such equable
intention as Lear brings to the business of abdication), self-
blame is perverted to angry sarcasm, and it falls to his servant
to preserve him from the menial office of correcting an insolent attendant of his daughter's. The anguish kept down
by native rumbustiousness peeps out in unconsidered asides
("No more of that, I have noted it well;" "A pestilent gall

to me!"). This pain, which constitutes the seriousness of
Lear's unregenerate state, is sharpened by the Fool's "act",
which at once mocks shallow "reason" and maddens Lear by
harping on his offence to reason in his surrender to his
daughters. Lear tolerates and seems to need this, in which we
can see the courage of his suffering even as he is pricked along
so that he should not be dragged down into chaos. "The
sweet and bitter Fool" in his backward glance, as it were, at
Polonius ("Have more than thou showest, / Speak less than
thou knowest"), with its regretful admission that "sense"
amounts to so much ("And thou shalt have more / Than
two tens to a score"), together with his pining for Cordelia,
melancholically acknowledges it his lot to be bound to the
"great wheel" of Lear. He reassures his master of his status
and helps turn his rage to suffering. The true pride of Lear's
heart is obscured by stubbornness, but it is part of his affliction to come to know the humility implicit in his plea, and
further to feel the indignity of his subjection to the worst that
may be in his children, as the Fool makes him feel it.

Goneril adopts a tone of pure disdain, and satisfies her real
irritation with contemptuous schoolmistress hectoring,
tormenting her father with his own wildness:

> But other of your insolent retinue
> Do hourly carp and quarrel ... .

She accompanies her grotesque insult of "redress" with
righteous indignation and a defiant arrogation to herself of
right: "Which else were shame, that then necessity / Will call
discreet proceeding." This triumphant sophistry is so evidently
satisfying to her soul that she is betrayed in her irritation and
her set determination not to own her father. Whether "other
of [Lear's] insolent retinue / Do hourly carp and quarrel"
does not signify (it is not past Lear to say like Goneril, "I'd
have it come to question"); it is a matter rather of the recognition, be it in kindness or in anger, of the claims of
another human being and a parent. Goneril withholds precisely this, and Lear cannot bear it that she should so coldly
repudiate any bond. Her frigidity galls him to outbreaks of

fury, the persistent appeal in which is that she cast off the character in which she stands revealed. In this he shows inability to acknowledge except in rage the guilt attaching to his parenthood. He cannot admit that this Goneril is his family:

> Does any here know me? This is not Lear.
> Does Lear walk thus, speak thus? Where are his eyes?
> Either his motion weakens, his discernings
> Are lethargied—Ha! Waking? 'T is not so?
> Who is it that can tell me who I am?

" Lear's shadow." The bitterly ironical supplication has nothing of guilt in it—the Fool is right to goad him. Nevertheless, when he lets Goneril gall him with reasons for denying him and castigate him for refractoriness, his words move towards the open confession of his anguish (" O reason not the need "), which in itself signifies release from the unavoidable deadlock. As Lear visibly suffers in his impotence to command respect Goneril loads on superfluous scorn:

> I do beseech you
> To understand my purposes aright.
> As you are old and reverend, should be wise ... .
> The shame itself doth speak
> For instant remedy ... .
> To be such men as may besort your age,
> Which know themselves and you.

It is Lear's evident frustration that puts the tremble of vindictive triumph into her voice, betraying her animosity. He responds by bringing it to the test, going so far as to " answer " her accusations, to defend the behaviour of his men and calling her undutiful for reproaching him with wilfulness.

He wields his claim on his daughters' duty in a different spirit from that of the insulting " Which of you shall we say doth love us most? " and almost confesses the error in blaming Cordelia for failing to support him with the implicit obedience he depended on: he speaks with self-pity of her " fault ",

and the lamentation is full of an anguished regret which is
the beginning of remorse:

> O most small fault,
> How ugly didst thou in Cordelia show,
> Which, like an engine, wrenched my frame of nature
> From the fixed place, drew from my heart all love,
> And added to the gall.

The anguish expresses Lear's pitiful complaint—and recognition—that Cordelia's refusal to comply made mad isolated
defiance incumbent on his pride, and brought about his exposure to the shameful cruelty of Goneril and Regan
("wrenched my frame of nature / From the fixed place").
There is no distinction in what he says between injustice and
guilt, and the involuntary suffering can only make him moan,
yet there is a mysterious compulsion in the pain, evident in
his clinging to it—his desire to sound it to the terrible depths
and not to turn away. Inevitably it causes Lear as much
distress to find he cannot master his suffering as it does to
uncover " these hard-hearts ", so that the bewilderment created
by his irrepressible defiance leaves him only with a dismayed
sense of having let himself down, of having let go his grip,
and made himself a prey to chaos:

> O Lear, Lear, Lear!
> Beat at this gate that let thy folly in
> And thy dear judgement out!

His choice here is responsibly to suffer what confronts him or
to lapse out in identification with the " contending elements "
and madness. His dire, anguished words do not strike us as
arbitrary or contingent: the pain of his impotence and helpless
subjection to suffering makes his wilfulness an authentic affliction. His attitude of " let come on me what will " may
seem reckless, but it is essentially the opposite of irresponsible.
He curses Goneril with sterility and she enjoys it (" let his
disposition have that scope / As dotage gives it") ; her response
characterizes his rage (his rage makes her say it), and the
curse is an admission that he is in pain and an implicit appeal:

> that she may feel
> How sharper than a serpent's tooth it is
> To have a thankless child!

To " come hither, and be confounded " (Job vi. 20) is deep
shame to him, not only because his pride is hurt but because it
blasts his faith. His tears make him a real father as they are
real tears: which is as they seduce Goneril to overt cruelty:

> That these hot tears, which break from me perforce,
> Should make thee worth them.

They infiltrate her satisfaction in her patrimony with the
unsought joy of annihilating her father, of denying his need
to be acknowledged in his wrath. She pleasantly hears his
exaggerated cries over the reduction of his retinue because,
like his improbable declaration of faith in her sister's " kindness " (" When she shall hear this of thee, with her nails /
She 'll flay thy wolvish visage "), they plead to be contradicted.
His huge dismay, his gestures of disbelief at Goneril's pre-
dictable pinching with the retinue, and his fond-hope assertion
of faith in Regan, are too innocent to be true. They in fact
show him shrewd enough about what he may expect from
his daughters who, the more they show their teeth, the more
he encourages them, effectually exposing their true natures.
Dismay always anticipates surprise in his dealings with them.
Goneril understands him, and just reiterates her " policy "
argument like a talisman against ill-luck as she quivers in the
thin satisfaction of a victory in meanness. With remarkable
protestation of the wisdom of caution, she gloats over his
tears:

> Safer than trust too far.
> Let me still take away the harms I fear,
> Not fear still to be taken.

Her falseness comes out in a ludicrous exaggeration which
compares with Lady Macbeth's arrogance— " He may enguard
his dotage with their powers, / And hold our lives in mercy "
—only she speaks for her own behoof, not her husband's,

whom she merely overbears in the elation of her liberty to do
as she will with Lear. She soars high above Albany in her
disdain to employ better than such reasons to discount him.
Lear, however, is rather cool at the termination of their exchange, instructing Kent carefully to "Acquaint my daughter
no further with anything you know than comes from her
demand out of the letter." Goneril ought not to have enjoyed
his "but yet have I left a daughter" so thoroughly. His
"trust" in Regan lasts about as long as his "astonishment"
at Goneril's hardness: he has no illusions about either of them:
he is merely going through with it. The Fool tells him nothing
new ("She's as like this as a crab's like an apple"), and his
prayer is only to stay sane long enough to run the course ("O
let me not be mad, not mad, sweet heaven! / Keep me in
temper; I would not be mad!")

Though he is clear about nothing but his bewilderment,
the character of Lear's anguish is such as to make it impossible for him but that he should suffer it to its conclusion, for
he is seriously up against it. It is otherwise with Gloucester,
whose sufferings befall him to his surprise, panic, chagrin
and subsequent fruitless enlightenment. Edmund's wickedness
answers to an habitual carelessness in his father, and at the end
turns to "some good I mean to do" with quite credible
suddenness. It is his amusement to set his victims to undo
themselves through foolishness—Gloucester, he is certain,
will not listen with incredulity to this stuff:

> Here stood he in the dark, his sharp sword out,
> Mumbling of wicked charms, conjuring the moon
> To stand auspicious mistress.

Edmund's sardonic estimate of his father's character is immediately confirmed by Gloucester's change of tune on "natural"
("and of my land, / Loyal and natural boy, I'll work the
means / To make thee capable"). The justice in Edmund's
cause gives a fairer face to his malign amusement than an
Iago's can have. Iago's malignity is counterpart of the necessity
in Othello's love and goes deeper with him. Edmund receives
no particular boost from what Gloucester shows of himself

which might turn his amused quickness to passion. The pleasure Goneril and Regan derive from annihilating their father in his very manhood is precisely of this kind: what they do to Lear characterizes both them and Lear. Their case bears relation to Iago's, not Edmund's. Goneril and Regan as much as Lear act in a passion: what makes both sisters fools of Edmund in his stage-villain holiday and what makes Lear by turns despairing and full of untrue conviction are shockingly related. Lear is out of his senses when he attaches himself with insistent identification to "mad Tom" (the role into which Edgar disappears with Gloucester-like simplicity and the imaginative facility of an actor, just before he nearly gives his father a heart-attack, "curing" him).

Lear is Gloucester's real salvation. So, too, in a minor way, Gloucester "saves" Edgar in the sense of confronting him with difficulties greater than those assumed by Edgar's guises and ministrations. Kent serves Lear most truly after he identifies himself unquestioningly with his cause and draws on himself misuse of the kind which maddens Lear. Kent takes it with the rough truculence of ordinary offence, a response denied the King by his pride. He criticises Lear, but also takes his part, deliberately, as a pledge of faith; it is a satisfaction to him to growl at the Steward in his open disgust, thereby challenging Cornwall to stop pretending respect for the King. He routs that nonsense, and Cornwall calls his plainness subtlety; but the subtlety is honest defiance of falsehood. You do not have to justify "Caius's" misbehaviour to see the honesty of Kent's defiance, or the warrant it has in Cornwall's and Regan's treatment of the King's messenger. Nor must one analyze his subtlety very far to understand why his usage at their hands brings him hope, with Cordelia's letter and the advent of the morning sun, as he sits in the stocks.

Kent's truculent pledge of himself to the King's interest earns him a "privilege" of anger which Edmund's superior verve, quick apprehension and animal spirits, unconnected to any such service, cannot gain him. Edgar has neither Edmund's self-interest nor his eagerness for adventure; he appears to act in resignation. Although he acts to evade capture, yet he does so with a peculiar, detached interest in imaginatively reducing himself to the lowest condition of man. His poetry of " poor, pelting villages " has a " documentary " lyricism strangely divorced from the reality of his predicament; a pat sincerity of attention to his theme. His device of acting the part of a Bedlam beggar seems to afford him the relief of a gratified wish to disappear; or, like Lear at one point, he sets himself to cope with the violence of the weather rather than the unfathomable meanings of the human soul:

> And with presented nakedness out-face
> The winds and persecutions of the sky.

The real desire is betrayed in his avowal that " Edgar I nothing am." Edgar, dodging his condition and yet far more in control than Lear, trivializes his danger and is unserious. In his well-meant readiness to let Lear and Gloucester attach themselves to the being he plays he looks shallow. Lear's enthusiasm for charity is all too like the fugitive's attention to beggars, which goes with a sincere belief in his own wisdom and right to tamper with men's agonies (" why I do trifle with him thus, is meant to cure him "). It is an instance of the philistinism to which Christ adverted his disciples when he admonished them that " ye have the poor always with you; but me ye have not always." (Matthew xxvi. 11) The effect of Edgar's therapy is merely to turn our attention from Lear's sentiments to what his having them might mean.

When Kent is put in the stocks he declines to soften the fact of his misuse. He makes Lear face it, protest his disbelief, demand contradiction, and get into the fury which alone can make him equal to the perfectly credible occurrence. Lear is furious, dismayed, wild—everything but surprised. " They durst not do 't. / They could not, would not do 't; 'tis worse than murder / To do upon respect such. violent outrage." Kent, in forcing Lear to face what has happened, ministers to him with a tact of true selfless respect for the pain and the courage he hears in his cry. Kent knows how hard it is for Lear to own the truth when he unrepentantly occasions him this distress. Lear's pain awakens respect in Kent and overcomes his desire to impose his wisdom on his errant master; in Gloucester too respect for Lear's suffering displaces lax satisfaction. In the Fool, who is ever wistful in the ironical glances he casts towards the world (Ariel is his spirit) Lear's plight awakens respect—and to Cordelia respect gives scope to unmake the nonsense she inherits and to honour her filial bond. " Winter's not gone yet if the wild geese fly that way " is the Fool's recognition both of the likelihood of Goneril's continuing hardness, and of the fight to follow when Lear faces the truth (" Where is this daughter?"). He is stirred by the prospect to pledge his loyalty in the ironic terms of his melancholically resigned act: " Let go thy hold when a great wheel runs down a hill, lest it break thy neck with following; but the great one that goes upward, let him draw thee after. When a wise man gives thee better counsel, give me mine again. I would ha' none but knaves <follow> it, since a fool gives it." Like Kent he knows Lear's "folly" yet mocks the world's " sense " which judges it so (" none but knaves "), and makes his sentimental, characteristically regretful pledge that he is not about to let go even if he should be drawn to ruin: " The knave turns fool that runs away: / The Fool no knave, perdy."

His followers keep Lear implacable so that he can meet Goneril's inflamed triumph of delight (" Every hour / He flashes into one gross crime or other. I 'll not endure it ") with the heat of rage ("Vengeance! plague! death! confusion! / Fiery? What quality?"). When she determinedly exagger- ates her indignation he meets her not with the despair of submission to her but with a passion root and branch with her own. In the darkness of passionate indirection he appeals to Regan's " kindness " as though to get the inevitable said, pleading in the face of all likelihood for her reassurance, daring her to deny him:

> Beloved Regan,
> Thy sister's naught. O Regan, she hath tied
> Sharp-toothed unkindness, like a vulture, here.

It is spoken with a sorry, and a very wary and awake, eye, for Lear could never in resignation appear so weakly pleading

before his child—justly, for he is slapped down without any
ado!:

> O sir, you are old;
> Nature in you stands on the very verge
> Of his confine. You should be ruled and led
> By some discretion ... .

Regan's performance is anticipated by him in his instruction
to Kent not to tell her about Goneril. It is no light matter for
Lear to believe his ears; he would stop them rather, obliterate,
deny, merely blast such heartlessness with the din of his fury,
whose pain is the one reality he always attaches himself to.
"This admiration", as Goneril calls his ironical posturings,
is the dark courage of Lear's soul, necessarily strange to his
conscious purposes. Herein lies the danger he runs in his
recklessness of "sense". The courage behind his rage begins
to turn to a recklessness of life and an increasing identification
with the elements of nature, whose neutral force is an inspiration to his weary soul. Believing that nature must repudiate
these abuses of human nature he calls upon the elements to
inflict condign punishment:

> You nimble lightnings, dart your blinding flames
> Into her scornful eyes! Infect her beauty,
> You fen-sucked fogs, drawn by the pow'rful sun
> To fall and blister her!

Commanding the god-like elements to take his part and blast
the unnatural abuse of filial ingratitude only takes the personal
edge of shame off his pain, and makes Lear verge upon relin-
quishing his faculties in an abandoned imaginative identity
with the elements. It is only his disbelieving, acid anger, irre-
pressibly prickly, which saves him. He draws scorn on himself
in fascinated disbelief:

> 'Tis not in thee
> To grudge my pleasures, to cut off my train,
> To bandy hasty words, to scant my sizes ...
> Thy half o' th' kingdom thou hast not forgot,

Wherein I thee endowed ... .
Regan. I pray you, father, being weak, seem so.

In his need to strike some spark off ordinary human decency
in his daughters, in a kind of fascination he allows his stipu-
lation for a hunting retinue to become the point of contention
between them, even to the point of offering to estimate them
in terms of what they will allow him there. They press his
apparent weakness cruelly and turn his all but open appeal for
a warm gesture, for the merest sign of recognition from them,
to shameful supplication, straitening their terms as he appears
to weaken until, disbelieving, Lear finds himself begging them
to stand by their least offer—he will go so far. And he proves
only that they do not want his offers, they want him out:

Regan.   What need one?
Lear. O reason not the need! Our basest beggars
      Are in the poorest things superfluous ...
            But for true need—
      You heavens, give me <that> patience—patience I
                                          need!

Patience to endure, that is, for he has now to know that it is
not for him to determine any sort of humane or human answer
by appeasement. His daughters simply choose not to listen,
Regan repeating her assertion that his men are " desperate ".
Lear tries to harden his face too, but the fury he summons
comes out vain-sounding and impotent; he is declared in his
need, the deadlock is broken by his admission of it and he
stands accomplished in his unadmitted object of being at the
mercy of his daughters' open hatred:

            Touch me with noble anger,
      And let not women's weapons, water-drops,
      Stain my man's cheeks. No, you unnatural hags,
      I will have such revenges on you both
      That all the world shall—— I will do such things—
      What they are yet I know not, yet they shall be
      The terrors of the earth!

King Lear (" Give me the map there. Know ...") pitifully
blustering like that before the triumph he has instilled into his
daughters is hardly to be called unregenerate still (unless you
would have him whine). At the latter end of his days he
stands in the hard obscurity of pain made unclear by contrary
convictions of righteousness and guilt; and makes himself an
object of pity, begging his daughters to be human beings, because he cannot bear it that they make him the father of fiends.

Lear wants the wildness of the elements, for their force
flatters his own painfully ineffectual force, and seems to redeem
in granting him a nobler perspective on his unmanning impotence to reach his daughters and establish any connection
with them or to penetrate their stony front at all. But in fact
he " runs unbonneted " on the heath, giving the world over
to negligence, in the context of Kent's solicitude, the Fool's
staunch, realistic loyalty, Gloucester's awakening courage, and
Cordelia's rescue. Anger makes him bid the sun draw up
vapours to poison Goneril, but the satisfaction this affords
vitiates his force and has him disclaiming humanity and declaring for the end of the world if it must be thus. The gratification this affords is just the relief of expending fury:

> And thou, all-shaking thunder,
> Strike flat the thick rotundity o' th' world,
> Crack Nature's moulds, all germens spill at once
> That makes ingrateful man!

The authentic note sounding through the proud, bitter joy of
disclaiming humanity—and distinguishing Lear's sympathies
from Edgar's in his hopeful forgery of beggardom—is Lear's
manifest need to mean it, which speaks through all the self-
delusion in his passion. " Edgar I nothing am " finds no echo
in Lear's soul: he gives himself to negligence with the world:
the cause, greater than he, is invincible, and the falseness in
his abandoned pride is neutralized as, harping on the theme of
filial ingratitude with increasingly unmeaning iteration, the
egotism is driven off, leaving real madness. The scornful
pride in the abdication challenge is worn away until Lear is
no longer at loggerheads with anyone, but isolated in his pain

tells over his grievances only to keep from foundering:

> I tax not you, you elements, with unkindness:
> I never gave you kingdom, called you children;
> You owe me no subscription.

Condescending now to the elements Lear, who can admit nothing, turns away from the fruitless strife to command obedience and the real, painful truth overcomes him. Yet it runs dangerously close to hysteria, this running to a standstill of incontrovertible rage:

> Then let fall
> Your horrible pleasure. Here I stand your slave,
> A poor, infirm, weak, and despised old man:
> But yet I call you servile ministers ... .

His desire to believe himself victim (with everyone else) of those impersonal elements thunder, wind, rain and incomprehensibly cruel children, clouds remorse and runs to madness. Lear, full of himself and eager to make amends to Bedlam beggars, defies the " great gods " only to learn that they are not to be bidden: his deep suffering comes with his profitless exultance, his fruitless patronising of Edgar, and the insanity brought on by his pride. The Fool's bawdy impinges on Lear's mind to draw his mind to a sharp sense of the challenge to his belief in himself as a man that his children constitute— yet that too runs to self-satisfaction and an unenlightened outburst against the false allure of women. Kent's fear is only Lear's mad hope, that " man's nature cannot carry / Th'affliction nor the fear." Lear is anything but afraid of the storm, which seems to him to objectify the obscure storm of his courage, to bring his suffering within the compass of willpower and understanding, and to permit his sense of injustice to reign:

> Let the great gods,
> That keep this dreadful pudder o'er our heads,
> Find out their enemies now. Tremble, thou wretch
> That hast within thee undivulged crimes

Unwhipped of justice ...
                    I am a man
More sinned against than sinning.

" Let the great gods " do this and that! But if it is characteristic of him that he receives guilt imperially, answering it as
though it came in deputation, still the general terms of his
address (prompted by the Fool's bawdy), " thou simular of
virtue / That art incestuous ", do reveal a critical frame of
mind, albeit in the style of Mark Antony owning to have been
a little high-handed with one of Caesar's messengers:

> ...I told him of myself, which was as much
> As to have asked him pardon.

For Lear magisterially to declare that all is not well in the
domain of man, and further that he is himself subject to the
universal affliction (" more sinned against than sinning " as
he calls his lot) is as much for him as to ask pardon. The
exculpatory formulation is the sop to his majesty which permits
him thus to acknowledge an inexpugnable malignancy in
which he bears a responsible share, and to get into the connection with his responsibility possible to his autocratic nature.
For, pre-empt blame as he would, Lear cannot bring himself peace by his protests at the universal inequity. There is
no finality in his address to the gods but only further indirection; his belief is sincere, but his words mislead him. The
true thing is the fight in Lear which makes him unable to lie
down; which although it remains unrealized by him speaks to
Kent and gives him the fire to resolve to brave Cornwall and
Regan and " force their scanted courtesy," to the Fool, who
can take his master's condescension so long as it results in his
accepting shelter, and to Gloucester, whose undemonstrative
decency is inspired: " If I die for it (as no less is threat'ned
me), the King, my old master, must be relieved." The wilder
Lear's conduct becomes, the less inclined any of his followers
is to question or turn from him or to offer the "concern" that
seeks to reform or " save ".

Lear gets a purchase on the " lesser malady " of the storm
to enable him to stand under the onslaught of the " greater ",
and in his albeit proprietary embrace of its violence, that inspires him with belief in a transcendent equity, really grapples
the pain of " filial ingratitude " to himself to fight it and
prevent it undoing him. The shame, unlike opposition which
is the family's incorrigible habit, has been fought for—is able
to be, now that the deadlock is resolved by his initiative into
declared conflict. He fights the storm, since he can take on
that:

When the mind's free
The body's delicate; <the> tempest in my mind
Doth from my senses take all feeling else
Save what beats there—filial ingratitude!

Defiance of the storm makes that admission possible, keeps
him on his feet, and gives him something he can do (" Pour
on, I will endure ") so that the world is kept alive and the
sore of " fililal ingratitude " well rubbed. It is an odd " exposure to feel what wretches feel " Lear practises catechizing
" mad Tom " with " Didst thou give all to thy daughters?
And art thou come to this?", but the pity he intends comes
out of his real personal affliction, and the intention does keep
that alive: the inspirational and no doubt short-lived attention
to " poor naked wretches " always insists on its correlative, his
responsibility, and likewise, when Lear is selfish in his ob-
session with daughters, he is here selfishly afflicted:

Is it the fashion that discarded fathers
Should have thus little mercy on their flesh?
Judicious punishment! 'T was this flesh begot
Those pelican daughters.

His decision that social wrongs ought to be righted, if there
is to be any justice, and his yet fruitless attention to Edgar
only brings it home to Lear that repentance is not to be " by
arrangement "—the seriousness of these inspirations of goodness is the desire which throws them up, which keeps the pain
alive until it is no longer to be borne; which causes the loss of

his wits as he clutches at these redeeming straws. It is for that that it is Lear who arrives at insanity and the benediction of Cordelia's love and not some falsification of Lear; as it is because of the absolute character of his desire that Macbeth arrived at nihility is—profoundly—Macbeth. His great disillusion does not strike Macbeth with the thought that he was a fool to have bothered and might as well have taken it easy, but is the bewildering truth towards which he has striven, and his creation. Hence the peculiar spiritedness with which he goes out to prove the worst in the last scenes. For there is something final and uniquely achieved, and in that at least beyond the paltering of passion and of fortune in "Tomorrow, and tomorrow, and tomorrow ..."; something, terribly, won and undeniable the winner. The grace bestowed upon Lear at the end is contingent upon, say, Cordelia's success in persuading the King of France to mount a British expedition. What is not subject to contingency and vicissitude, because it belongs to the character of his volition, is the desire in Lear, there in his general demeanour towards what he finds he has to do. If his conception of the grace of Cordelia's love at the end is half-fanciful, that cannot destroy the connection between the wonder in his "Look there, look there" and what he has done to make it possible.

Gloucester's sovereign service of Lear having denied the apparent unseriousness which permitted him to believe, in a panic, in Edgar's "treachery", he is left distraught, not knowing how to live any more. His horrible injury is inflicted upon him as a result of his ignorance and credulous disposition, which his courage more than redeems; even so, he does not have Lear's sense of what he is taking on, and his valour lies in his not in any case making that his question. It reverses his unbelief in Edgar, yet neither his humility nor the proof of his loyalty made by the injury he suffers comes with the necessity that Lear's less tangible suffering exhibits. The blinding of Gloucester powerfully emphasizes that whether Lear's cry is a genuine one or not does not depend on what he brings on himself—the good or the bad—or on whether it is heard. The courage in his wilful suffering gives it its significance, a significance that it possesses even if he himself misses it or those who respond to it misinterpret it. Lear is never enlightened, and his moment of truth is a moment of pure wonder, guaranteeing nothing beyond itself; but Gloucester, after action, is but bewildered and lost—there is nothing that stings him as the meaning of his daughters' hatred stings Lear, nothing like that to keep him alive—to sustain life itself, and to sustain belief:

> Thou sayest the King grows mad; I'll tell thee, friend,
> I am almost mad myself. I had a son,
> Now outlawed from my blood: he sought my life
> But lately, very late: I loved him, friend,
> No father his son dearer: true to tell thee,
> The grief hath crazed my wits.

What Gloucester finds when he comes terribly to himself in his encounter with Cornwall is not so strange to him. The spring of his courage is its connection, not accidental, with the collapse of Lear's confident identification with " poor naked wretches " into nonplussed, frank puzzlement expressed in open queries: " Then let them anatomise Regan; see what breeds about her heart. Is there any cause in nature that makes these hard-hearts?" Gloucester makes his sacrifice just when the King is most vulnerable, his pride baffled, and his pugnacious independence about to subside behind frank puzzlement at life. It is the occasion, too, of Goneril's and Regan's final unmasking. As soon as they no longer need to keep up a face of haughty forebearance they fall naturally into a double-act of provocation to cruelty, so that in the last moment of his sighted existence Gloucester sees, in Regan's unreined passion, what Lear is up against, a viciousness in his children which fills Gloucester with pity and admiration for him: " Yet, poor old heart, he holp the heavens to rain." The spectacle of Lear's stubbornness in this light overcomes Gloucester's sense of imminent peril with wonder, and in upshot he is disabused of his conviction of Edgar's treachery. Regan, who thinks to hurt him by disclosing it to him, merely shows the blood in her eyes. But like Enobarbus overcome by Antony's magnanimity Gloucester finds shame only to lose

his desire to live. Lear, in contrast, seeks ever to meet his
shame, despite that the character of the trying always obscures
the shame.

Edgar's desire to lose himself is made to look trifling by
Lear's wilful exposure to the worst that can befall him: what
should pass through his mind on hearing how his subterfuge
occasioned his father's despair?

Gloucester. I' th' last night's storm I such a fellow saw,
Which made me think a man a worm. My son
Came then into my mind.

Gloucester's enlightenment only leaves him lost and tired; his
"As flies to wanton boys are we to th' gods; / They kill us for
their sport" goes with his suicide attempt as an avowal of
hopelessness; for his restored courage is no new thing to him
but matter of course; he never regards it; it leaves him where
he was, only disabused of some unpleasant convictions. Like
Enobarbus, Gloucester has no direction once the connection
with his master is broken—once his master's direction is lost.
It characterizes Gloucester's spirit that he is quite cast down
by the spectacle of Lear wandering mad, unequal to Lear's
wholeness of heart, and catches the sense of universal wrong
maddening Lear only sincerely to take his leave of the world.
The following reflections are not made with the intention to
do anything about them or, like Lear, with any intention
towards the anguish they come from, but in farewell:

Heavens, deal so still!
Let the superfluous and lust-dieted man,
That slaves your ordinance, that will not see
Because he does not feel, feel your power quickly;
So distribution should undo excess,
And each man have enough. Dost thou know Dover?

Gloucester's sincerity, Lear's *terribilità*—the harm on the
former's face insists on the character of the distinction, that
it is not contingent on what befalls or on conscious intention.
The play shows very clearly at this juncture, with Gloucester

and Lear both in their ways broken and out of the fight, the different human beings they are, and—marvellously in the counterpoise of Lear's willed and intangible suffering with Gloucester's involuntary and physical suffering—the greater desire in Lear, the spirit infallible in all the confusion of his life.

The desire in Lear is betraying like Macbeth's or Othello's and causes him fruitless elation, darkening understanding. The desire in Goneril and Regan causes them elation, but is itself fruitless: the elation thinly covers chaos. Edmund spurns his brother's sincere goodness in order to enjoy his superiority over those whom, in his amorality, he is able to make his dupes. When Goneril, elated by cruelty, offers him herself, she is mocked:

> I must change arms at home and give the distaff
> Into my husband's hands. This trusty servant
> Shall pass between us: ere long you are like to hear
> (If you dare venture in your own behalf)
> A mistress's command. Wear this. Spare speech:
> Decline your head: this kiss, if it durst speak,
> Would stretch thy spirits up into the air.
> Conceive, and fare thee well.

The thrill of command taught her by her triumph over her father makes her foolish in her passion, so that she does not see the amusement in Edmund's face as he accepts her various bestowals. Edmund—"Yours in the ranks of death!"—is not altogether where she thinks she has him: his aloofness, a pride itself, is too precious to trade for a woman or a cause. He is long instructed in it by, for instance, his father's assumption that he, his bastard son, could not feel towards him as a son. Cornwall's use and Goneril's disposition of him are alike contemptuous and make only for contempt: the desire in her admiration of him here is really just Goneril trying out her new liberty to dispose her favours anywhere she chooses:

> O, the difference of man and man!
> To thee a woman's services are due;
> < My fool usurps my body. >

There is nothing for Edmund to hear in that but Goneril's arrogant disdain of her husband and exultant self-satisfaction, together with a certitude of his reciprocal desire that interests and amuses him. Goneril's condescension to Edmund compared with Lady Macbeth's fiery, scornful devotion to Macbeth makes the distinction between the vanity of lust and the pride of love. Her conceited superiority to Albany is of the same substance as her beckonings to Edmund, and in both instances the opposite of Lady Macbeth's instrumental scorn. It is plainly stimulated by jealousy, to cover with elation an inner hell, Goneril's possession by which is betrayed in her turn of speech here as she speaks of her sexual hopes:

> But being widow, and my Gloucester with her,
> May all the building in my fancy pluck
> Upon my hateful life.

Disdain for Albany and desire for Edmund cover poisonous loathing and fear of her life and can provide but a fruitless satisfaction, not unlike Lear's outburst against the betrayal of sexual desire. Goneril has nothing for Edmund that Regan has not, and her triumph is desperate.

Cordelia is brought to a clarity of soul, her sisters to a fury. In the satisfaction of their cruelty Goneril and Regan are lost, abandoned to contingency and what is to be had in a free-for-all. The chaos seething under Goneril's elated demeanour comes out in an irritable, drear will to wrest enjoyment from the destruction they have wrought; she is dependent on the success of that and her happiness is bounded by its possibilities, and is thus in the opposite case to Cordelia, whose attentive sympathy lets her see her father as he is and help him:

> Alack, 'tis he! Why, he was met even now
> As mad as the vexed sea, singing aloud,
> Crowned with rank fumiter and furrow-weeds,
> With hardocks, hemlocks, nettles, cuckoo-flowers,
> Darnel, and all the idle weeds that grow
> In our sustaining corn.

Cordelia is able to contemplate her father in his abandoned
identification with the elements that he had attempted to recruit once to help him defy "unnatural" humanity to abuse
him. She is recognizably the daughter whose angry sense
held her from assenting to her father's whim; if at the end
she pays more than "those duties as are right fit", the love
she knows is different from Kent's ("My master calls me, I
must not say no"). She obeys the biblical injunction to
"honour thy father". Edgar's muddled sincerity is actually
more effective than Cordelia's righteous love—she does not
save her father's life: but Edgar's assurance jars with Gloucester's final seriousness. For Gloucester, collected enough to
remember to tip his conductor, is in deadly earnest here:

> O you mighty gods!
> This world I do renounce, and in your sights
> Shake patiently my great affliction off.

The distance between Edgar's confidence in his "cure" and
Cordelia's understanding of what her father is come to
measures the seriousness of Lear's and Gloucester's respective
suffering, what it is and what it makes possible. "Alive, or
dead?"—does the question make Edgar's heart stop? But if
it is touch and go and a muddle, Edgar's cure being very
nearly fatal, he does save Gloucester from giving up the ghost,
and by a good fortune as much his own as Gloucester's. Yet
it is not entirely Edgar's fault if he is afraid to identify himself to his father even when Gloucester is wandering eyeless.

Gloucester, weary of the world, is pitiable, but Lear out of
his senses makes a terrible human spectacle. The conviction
abides to mislead him that in the storm he forced the truth,
but his reiteration of that is painfully mingled with a sardonic
self-deflation that seems to arise of itself: "When the rain
came to wet me once and the wind to make me chatter, when
the thunder would not peace at my bidding, there I found 'em,
there I smelt 'em out! Go to, they are not men o' their words;
they told me I was everything; 'tis a lie—I am not ague-
proof." The storm brought on his rheumatism! In that vein
he guys his majesty—"I pardon that man's life"—half in a

mood of "let it go all", half in mockery of the world's expectations, which would have the King bear the responsibility
yet would use him with flattery. With his outburst of sexual
loathing he would knowingly disclaim belief in the "sostegno
e gloria d'umanità" (*Don Giovanni*, Act III) and, as the
parent of such children as these, decry desire's mean betrayal.
His sexual life has amounted to so much. Even so, there is an
element of shame in the energy with which he expends his
detestation; a defiant refusal, at least, at all to cover up the
foulness he has brought into being. His pride holds him
resolutely opposed to his daughters, "what they are", and
incapable of decrying himself as "centaur" too (as, exhibiting
a different pride, Don Giovanni might happily enough have
done): yet at the same time the need to maintain the opposition and the refusal keeps alive the shame their natures must
cause him. His diatribe against women is in this way as
irresistibly an expression of Lear as Macbeth's "tomorrow,
and tomorrow, and tomorrow" is an expression of Macbeth,
and as unenlightening:

> Down from the waist they are centaurs,
> Though women all above.
> But to the girdle do the gods inherit,
> Beneath is all the fiend's.
> There's hell, there's darkness, there is the sulphurous pit;
> Burning, scalding, stench, consumption: fie, fie, fie,
>   pah, pah!
> Give me an ounce of civet; good apothecary, sweeten
>   my imagination: there's money for thee.

It is too much Goneril's drear exultation, too indulgently close
to her confession, "my hateful life"; his awful glee of "there
I smelt 'em out", too much her deluded elation, rather
frightening in its darkness. Yet if Lear remains in the dark,
he is not damned, but his will to "make things change, or
cease" persists, whilst the women are nowhere, lost in a frenzy
of set hatred. His awful insane loathing is part of Lear's
tragic will, for his despair of how the world is constituted has

its roots in guilt over the world he has made, and if the loathing affords relief, it is only in the agony it affords:

Gloucester. O, let me kiss that hand!
Lear. Let me wipe it first, it smells of mortality ... .

King Lear railing on the hypocrisy of mortal authority
(" Thou rascal beadle, hold thy bloody hand ") is close
enough, for all his accusation of the lot of mortal man, to
self-castigation. The lord of justice bewails the frailty of all
flesh, and his savage joy in giving it all to perdition hurts,
because he is responsible: it is not like Gloucester's sad farewell, nor Timon of Athens' obliterating scorn, who holds all
the while trump cards of exile and suicide. Lear intends nothing beyond seeing it out (scathingly) and his prayer is
always for strength to endure:

> Thou must be patient. We came crying hither;
> Thou know'st the first time that we smell the air
> We wawl and cry.

His native fierceness runs to poignant self-mockery and a wry
ironical posturing addressed to a life that has been lived—
far less than anything enacted by Hamlet is it to be questioned:

> No seconds? All myself?
> Why, this would make a man <,> a man of salt< >
> To use his eyes for garden water-pots,
> Ay, and laying autumn's dust.

Lear is undeniable where it is not his personal pride alone that
speaks, but he looks with irony upon the usage of " the great
image of authority", the King, himself; where he is inconsol-
able, despite the reverence and yearning pity of his followers,
though near to or in tears; and where in his madness—" Come,
an you get it you shall get it by running. Sa, sa, sa, sa "—
he commands only respect.

The dignity he pushes away at the last, finding his own
majesty insupportably poignant, is returned to him by Cordelia's loving respect that acknowledges him in his pain. Lear

awakens to hear her clear enunciation of the human due he
demanded, in his daughter's recognition of his pain as his own
and not as what may be estimated or guessed at. Hers is a
deeply human voice in the chaos of his abandonment:

> Mine enemy's dog,
> Though he had bit me, should have stood that night
> Against my fire; and wast thou fain, poor father,
> To hovel thee with swine and rogues forlorn,
> In short and musty straw?

The protest in her words is the protest of common humanity,
her " my " meaning " anyone's ". The bewilderment to which
Lear has brought himself is blessed by a common truth. But
she cannot make him valiant against the world again, since
he can only accept his truth now as something given. It ap-
proves the suffering he underwent. It means agony too; it
shows him the eternal, unappeased necessity, and that such
grace is forever to be sought:

> You do me wrong to take me out o' th' grave:
> Thou art a soul in bliss; but I am bound
> Upon a wheel of fire, that mine own tears
> Do scald like molten lead.

Her compassion may be an accomplishment of his, but, if
mercy has to do with relief from pain, it is hardly merciful:
he is all but unequal to hearing it:

> Where have I been? Where am I? Fair daylight?
> I am mightily abused; I should e'en die with pity
> To see another thus.

Gratitude he may feel for the redemption of his sense of things
—but his new sense of things is wondering and uncompre-
hending. He is " mightily abused " by such a certitude now.
He is never to share Cordelia's determination to take on
" these sisters " again, and the wrath has passed from his
demands. He desires now only that a fancied state of bliss
should continue.

Goneril's jealousy is matched by Regan's, and it deprives her of dignity: "But have you never found my brother's way / To the fore-fended place?": and displays the essential contempt of their desire, the uneasiness of their conviction that their attentions must flatter Edmund. Perhaps it is Edmund's careless acquiescence that stimulates both. There is a defensive note in his avowal of self-interest, too, an unease about the real superiority of his pose of detachment that makes his last-minute inspiration of goodness credible enough: "Each jealous of the other, as the stung / Are of the adder ... for my state / Stands on me to defend, not to debate." He begins to distaste his dependence for his satisfaction on Goneril's and Regan's unhandsome passion, and " some good I mean to do " comes out with obvious relief at the least in brushing the sisters off his coat. Their desire holds him down to a subterfuge in the end tiresome.

Cordelia, a prisoner, is fired by her old *hauteur* (" Shall we not see these daughters and these sisters?") while Lear, beyond all that, contemplates bliss. Retribution is for the living. But his fancy of a charmed life of god-like supervision of mankind, in prison, is as far from reality as his conviction that he distrained the truth of the gods, outfacing the violent weather, quite unenlightened—and yet given expression in a true voice of Lear's, splendidly passionate in its magnanimous certitude:

> Upon such sacrifices, my Cordelia,
> The gods themselves throw incense. Have I caught thee?
> He that parts us shall bring a brand from heaven
> And fire us hence like foxes. Wipe thine eyes;
> The good-years shall devour them, flesh and fell,
> Ere they shall make us weep! We'll see 'em starved first.
> Come.

Who but Job's Comforters would deny him? His conviction of his capacity, in its passion, is as final a truth for him as Macbeth's drear dawning; what he has made; what he is now because of what he has done. Cordelia is hanged, and Lear, accusing the heart of man, is unanswerable:

Howl, howl, howl! O, you are men of stones!
Had I your tongues and eyes, I'd use them so
That heaven's vault should crack! She's gone for ever.
I know when one is dead, and when one lives;
She's dead as earth.

His is the last anguish, always clouded—" I might have saved her "—but still perfect wonder, Lear's wonder at his life distilled, at the moment of his death and for that moment, into the regard he fastens upon Cordelia's lips. The vain vestigial fury and accusation concludes upon pure wonder:

> Thou 'lt come no more,
> Never, never, never, never, never!
> Pray you, undo this button. Thank you, sir.
> Do you see this? Look on her! Look—her lips!
> Look there, look there!

CHAPTER VI

Cleopatra's Masterpiece

The exasperated soldiers of Antony grumble about their "Mars"; Enobarbus burbles replete with satisfaction in the Egyptian interlude; and Antony finds his pleasure intolerable. Irresistibly the lover Cleopatra flatteringly mocks him for, with a large air he declines to return her "wrangling", draws her seductive taunts on himself, and keeps them both fed. In the face of her laughter he stoutly maintains the figure of Antony, devotee of Love, the improbability of which is the great joke of their love talk:

Cleopatra. If it be love indeed, tell me how much.
Antony. There's beggary in the love that can be reckoned.
Cleopatra. I'll set a bourn how far to be beloved.
Antony. Then must thou needs find out new heaven,

new earth.

He is serious and so (enjoying her power to make him so) is she, there is a real intimacy, yet with no peace in it but an uneasy gratification eternally to be pursued. They try their exalted attunement out and get a heady boost of superiority, then stand apprehensive about what it is they have. The teasing laugh in Cleopatra's voice beckons Antony, who rises to the appeal in her challenge to "Tell me" with serious protestation. But the game of cultivated desire is a deadlock, beyond which nothing materializes.

The Alexandrian court is Cleopatra's exotic garden where she cultivates Love. Wise and cunning and very complacent, she is so full of Love and its varieties she is in essence un-worldly—of all things. Devoted in the "infinite variety" of her nature she pursues Love's ends with truly regal sufficiency, perfectly un-self-interested. For as for love, that commodity is but her stock in trade ("us that trade in love"). If Antony were able to deal solely on the terms she proffers there need be

no more to his attraction to her than gallant homage to a
" wonderful piece of work "—Enobarbus, the *simpatico* enthusiast, does her no great injustice with the phrase. But Enobarbus pays with his life for his beguilement, and Antony's
need to "break off", his yearning to have back his men's
esteem and his self-command (fatally sentimental as it is in
reference to Enobarbus) is so hard of fulfilment because in the
very "dotage" of the love-game, in the irritable satisfaction of
indulged and teased-out passion, a necessity establishes itself
that peremptorily countermands the promptings of honour.
Cleopatra's gusto for being made love to, what Philo the
Roman calls " a gypsy's lust ", comes from the eternal require-
ment that her " infinite variety " be served and admired—
answered, whether with peace or with war. Antony more than
acquiesces in her thrill of possession when he lets himself be
captivated with a cultivated gesture, infinitely repeated; he is
inspired with a disdain to count the cost that leaves him irritable to actuality.

His wife's death makes the reproach of unmanly neglect he
needs in order to set about challenging Cleopatra's terms of
love. His impatience to be off and managing affairs is from
deeper self-dissatisfaction than arises from neglect of his office:
his pre-emptive expedition, that nonplusses Pompey and rouses
Caesar to enmity, is undertaken with surprising decision. All
the while, gratified in her power to make him impossibly
superb ("I bind, / On pain of punishment, the world to weet
/ We stand up peerless"), Cleopatra rests serene in her provoc-
ativeness; how well she knows Antony and can rely on him
shows in the amusing falseness of all her " storms and tem-
pests ", the pure assumption in the eternal mocking joke.
Antony's avowals—

> Here is my space.
> Kingdoms are clay: our dungy earth alike
> Feeds beast as man: the nobleness of life
> Is to do thus

—she accepts as gestures of loyalty to her exoticism, un-
questioning solidarity with her enterprise to ignore the world.
She hoots, so to speak, with laughter—and waves back,

" wrangling " to draw him on and make him worse. Portentous unreality hovers about them which, causing a real prickliness of the one to the other, her sharp taunts and his annoyance, makes, of their anxiety to keep it up, real love. It is intolerable that the arrogant splendour they make with each other should be an indulgence and no more: the more fantastical and proud it is the more it goads Antony despite himself to make it a reality or nothing. Suddenly he is very politically effective, whilst Enobarbus and the Romans generally think he is engaged merely in an escapade.

" Love seeketh only self to please " (Blake) is true of Cleopatra only as she poses in her serenity and waits for Antony—assuming in all her behaviour towards her adversary that he waits on love. She, personally, asks nothing of love (compare Desdemona's exulting joy), but lets it blossom, or seek its pleasure as it will. Antony, on the other hand, is temperamentally reliant on the warm personal appeal of his magnetism and on the reassurance of the regard in which he is held: he has not her aloofness to the world and to emulate her regal sufficiency has to let go of a necessary assurance. The devotion that allows him to do so finally awakens in her a real admiration for him and a sympathy with his rage against the gods and herself which deepens the pride of her cultivation into love. Antony obeys his desire to suffer the last extremity of passion and make it real when, upon hearing the news of his wife's death, he bestirs himself, indulging a feeling sigh and a sentimental, at bottom insincere, regret:

> O , then we bring forth weeds
> When our quick <winds> lie still, and our ills told us
> Is as our earing.

Emotionally demonstrative, prone to misgiving and to wear his heart upon his sleeve, to stand back from a situation and to regard it with the common eye, what Antony really argues himself into with his self-reproof is getting some impetus for action to resolve the genuine irritant, the lapse of time leaving him incapable of action and subject to the contingency of events.

The hand could pluck her back that shoved her on.
I must from this enchanting queen break off.

The resolution is cast as a reproach to his subservience, but
what he really means must be judged by what he immediately
does, which is to get his relations with Cleopatra on to a possible footing—not "break off". His dissatisfaction with himself only comes about when they importune him from home,
and is a form of annoyance—he would sooner they left him
alone, and he reproaches himself with unmanly neglect as he
bestirs himself to put an end to an impossible situation. His
intention is to come to Cleopatra as her equal in free independence and so no longer have to dance to her delicious, intolerable tune; only being Antony he has first to catch sight of
his own indolence in the behaviour of Enobarbus—only then
does he put it off and go straight ahead moved by a stern
determination to reform. Enobarbus's quips about "members
to make new" wives and why Antony is bound to stay (Cleopatra's business "wholly depends on [his] abode") belong
to the military swagger and just help Antony into his familiar
tunic so that, like Tolstoy's Count Vronsky in barracks, he
feels at home again and equal to anything. Antony resolves
to leave and deal with the nuisance, Pompey, feeling his old
self and an emperor still. But when he has dealt with Pompey,
and concluded some business which does interest him, he is
back just as he reassures Cleopatra he will be.

Her practitioner's concern for her technique ("What should
I do, I do not?") disarms Cleopatra's malice as she keeps her
slightly ponderous, lover ("How, my love?") on the stretch.
Her devotion to the hot-house culture absorbs her, complac-
ently accustomed as she is to using her consorts with too
amazing cheek. What should be emotion—jealousy and anger
at their parting—is expressed with a chuckle and an appreciative eye on the performance. Her very desire to hurt is cultivated, not in affectation but simply in right royal indifference. For as long as she remains her unapproachable self,
which knowing perfectly its effect she would never be anything
but, Antony cannot leave her: her existence is a flattery to his
soul. Cleopatra possesses her soul with all the pride of a

Hamlet, only she goes beyond Hamlet to fashion her world according to the gifts and vision of her nature. "The holy priests / Bless her when she is riggish." She is possessed of royal assumption and even in the triviality of dalliance her appetite is fed for the sake of the joy of the day, whilst towards the future she preserves a perfect *sang-froid*. She does not cloy the appetite she feeds. Where she might well be desolated, made downcast or (like romantic heroines) resolute for death at Antony's marriage, her fury leaps to confront what with perfect faith she takes for the spirit of antagonistic love-making in the move. She is utterly without unworthy suspicion that in this she is anything other than provoked. Antony announces that Fulvia's death is the last straw and he must be off, and she is immediately superb with scoffing ridicule on behalf of ill-used woman:

> O, never was there queen
> So mightily betrayed!

Her satisfaction violated, she merely enjoys the spectacle of Antony anxious for his reputation and resolute for honour. He hears his departure received with this mock mockery and groans. He will be back. She taunts him with his vows not unfairly to hold him to them but to madden him with the flavour of their mutual extravagance:

> When you sued staying,
> Then was the time for words: no going then;
> Eternity was in our lips and eyes,
> Bliss in our brows' bent; none our parts so poor
> But was a race of heaven.

Her sarcasm is referred to a vital and highly particular imagination of human love. It is full of the poetry of the nature she is. It recalls in this Hamlet's "Hyperion to a satyr, so loving to my mother, / That he might not beteem the winds of heaven / Visit her face too roughly", only it is more nearly related to the sensual reality than this. Laughing at them both, and bitter enough, she maintains an essential indifference to the might-have-been, and is mocking and elusive in her passion,

appealingly suggestive. She does not cloy with emotionality
but in a moody, inconsequential attachment to desire gestures
at their love-making in order to hurt, assuming his departure
to be a " move " aimed at her which she answers in the spirit
of the fight. And in a sense her response makes it such, whatever Antony intends. She turns all his intentions to so much
male guff, mere contemptible reasons, and enjoys his seriousness:

> O, my oblivion is a very Antony,
> And I am all forgotten.

Whilst she is so full of possibilities and so indifferent (the
possibilities " wholly depend on [his] abode "...) all his explanations to her and to himself are useless. Nothing has
changed, her farewell is none but a love-beck to which he responds in the end with a Metaphysical conceit in which both
recognize the right language:

> Our separation so abides and flies,
> That thou, residing here, goes yet with me,
> And I, hence fleeting, here remain with thee.
> Away!

Yet Cleopatra ought rather to have heeded his urgency than
approved the gesture with which he prepares his way.

Caesar, righteous with the ideal spirit of the empire which
he embodies, senses Antony's impatience. Sniffing his opportunity in Fulvia's death and Antony's inevitable discomfiture
at it he calls out to him, " Leave thy lascivious wassails," re-
collecting his past exploits with a vibration of true desire, to
know Antony. Caesar admires Antony in desire to annihilate
him. Antony's slack sensual abandon Caesar does not understand and chastely distastes—disapproving, Antony's appeal
for him betrays fascination and desire to take him on, his
equal whom his spine resists. This opposition to Antony of
the spirit of Rome (which it takes an Antony to bring out) is
counterpart to what in Antony's own nature makes it impossible to dally for ever on Cleopatra's terms. Not the reproach of duty with which he can always cope, but his Roman

energy, so essentially opposite to Egypt's high, cultured voluptuousness (for all that, being barbered ten times over, the spirited Antony goes to the feast), goads him to and fro across the ancient Mediterranean world in troubled conflict. Caesar's callow high-mindedness is an aspect of the Roman sense of destiny, the empire-builder's arrogation of righteousness. Its animosity to the possibilities of the Cleopatrian assumption impinges more nearly on Antony than the republicanism of Venice does on Othello, and in the end moves Antony more or less desperately to make love, final and fatal, of the Eastern dream. Othello is all " for love " too, but Antony is consciously so, in the end, out of defiance.

For, despite her belief to the contrary, it is not to the tricky, satisfied Queen of Love he means to return. In Antony's absence " on her service " Cleopatra luxuriates in the gratification of her desire to bind him to love, her greatest conquest so far under the banner of Venus. She feeds on the delicious pain of parting (on " such sweet sorrow " not at all, but " most delicious poison "), and conjures the fascination she must have for Antony, " black " as she is, since " wrinkled deep in time " " with Phoebus' amorous pinches "—teasing out the languor of her content with desire, inflamed and denied:

> O Charmian!
> Where think'st thou he is now? Stands he or sits he?
> Or does he walk? or is he on his horse?
> O happy horse, to bear the weight of Antony!
> Do bravely, horse! for wots't thou whom thou mov'st?
> The demi-Atlas of this earth, the arm
> And burgonet of men. He's speaking now,
> Or murmuring," Where's my serpent of old Nile?"
> For so he calls me.

Whilst in fact Antony has set his face away, Cleopatra figures to herself his dotage of doting on her and the addition he makes to the conquests of one who has been a " morsel for a monarch ", before whom " great Pompey / Would stand and make his eyes grow in [her] brow." The suggestiveness in the phrase conveys the female triumph and amusement at male vanity, " greatness ": " great Pompey "! She does not do her lovers down, but proudly recalling them congratulates herself on them, her dominion over and proprietorship of their pride:

> How much unlike art thou Mark Antony! ...
> How goes it with my brave Mark Antony?

And Mark Antony obligingly sends pearls and vows, all in good part. Whereupon it is " O heavenly mingle "—she recites his superlative specification (he would not this and that &c.). Airily brandishing Antony's " greatness ", which just sets off her power to bind and loose men's souls, Cleopatra savours the piquancy of her claim to have been a morsel for a monarch: who eats whom? The humour of the " twenty several messengers " she has sent after Antony accords perfectly with this mood of amused complacence. She is just asking for it. For it is a perfectly impossible " my " she indulges in discounting all her former avowals in order to display her perfect freedom to say what she will:

> By Isis, I will give thee bloody teeth,
> If thou with Caesar paragon again
> My man of men

—particularly as she believes it. Charmian's sly irony flatters her as she wants, to elicit her disclaimer:

> My salad days,
> When I was green in judgement, cold in blood,
> To say as I said then.

" If you enjoyed that, watch this." Such a very satisfactory female applecart just asks to be tipped over, and Antony's marriage to Caesar's sister supplies the demand: Cleopatra can watch that. After that he is straight back.

The rebel Pompey rides on a high tide of power and popularity and is a serious threat to Rome until he learns that his

revolt has stirred Mark Antony, whereupon it shrinks with
him to a matter of saving face. Antony, however, does not
mind Pompey; he quite likes him, and would probably as soon
give him the fight he seeks if his mind were not elsewhere.
Antony's singlemindedness incidentally finishes the ambitious
and successful Pompey. It is not because he goes to the con-
ference bent on appeasing Caesar. Enobarbus takes his cue
from his master when he spurns Lepidus's suggestion that he
should persuade Antony to placate Caesar.

Antony, purposefully man-to-man, gains the initial advantage of Caesar, who does not care to display his disapprobation
of the older man's " I ... did want / Of what I was i'th'
morning." Yet he silences Enobarbus who would introduce
an open levity into the proceedings, wanting to play politics
right enough, only on his own terms. Both principals understand each other's fundamental opposition too well to waste
time in personality conflicts. The suggestion that Antony
marry Octavia comes as no surprise to anyone—or at least is
so close to what each wants at heart, a close and dangerously
fragile connection, that neither betrays a flicker of misgiving
lest he should seem to waver in the " eyeball to eyeball "
confrontation. What an Enobarbus can see in a moment in
the proposed marriage, that " that which is the strength of
their amity shall prove the immediate author of their vari-
ance ", neither mentions; only the silence of both regarding
their use of the third party, Octavia, betrays the tension between them. They control their hostility and get straight to
the point, which is the conditions for their duel.

In contrast to their wary dealing the subordinates, with a
merely professional interest, enjoy an immediate *camaraderie*.
Enobarbus, still full of the wonders of the East, relates Cleopatra's seduction of Antony with the relish of a connoisseur.
The memory of the famous spectacle fills him with enjoyment: he is a good deal impressed, though perfectly equal to a
performance: " I will tell you." He is impressed, but laugh-
ingly; impressed by the extravagant scale, the uninhibited
imagination and grand sweep of Cleopatra's spectacle; appreciative as a connoisseur and man of the world, but not over-
awed. His sophistication recognizes the challenge in the grand

gesture, the offer and the dare, and his listeners are to contemplate Cleopatra's wonderfully accomplished style, in which she is unapproachable, and admire Antony's spirit:

> our courteous Antony,
> Whom ne'er the word of "No" woman heard speak,
> Being barbered ten times o'er, goes to the feast,
> And for his ordinary, pays his heart
> For what his eyes eat only.

His picture of the famous meeting is full of willing admiration and wonder at the transforming creation of the queen:

> The barge she sat in, like a burnisht throne
> Burned on the water: the poop was beaten gold;
> Purple the sails, and so perfumed that
> The winds were love-sick with them; the oars were silver,
> Which to the tune of flutes kept stroke and made
> The water which they beat to follow faster,
> As amorous of their strokes.

Even so it exhibits Enobarbus's confidence that, even if it was enough to knock him off his feet, he knows what kind of thing it was: and there is some justice in the presumption. Their own grand gesture does at first fascinate Antony and Cleopatra; and it is this that Antony starts to make change, or cease. Until which Agrippa's crude summary,

> Royal wench!
> She made great Caesar lay his sword to bed:
> He ploughed her, and she cropped,

has the justification of being Cleopatra's own tone, vulgarized; just what she hugs herself with pleasure for, in Egypt, as he speaks. Enobarbus, however, has seen her, and his spirit is touched by a greater magic than a grand flair—this really is sublime in her, even when it comes out in public exhibitions and the cultivation for their own sake of a range of wiles:

Never, he will not:
Age cannot wither her, nor custom stale
Her infinite variety: other women cloy
The appetites they feed, but she makes hungry
Where most she satisfies: for vilest things
Become themselves in her, that the holy priests
Bless her when she is riggish.

His emphatic certainty that she is a nonpareil in humanity, whose very languor and wantonness shine with inexhaustible life, transcends the connoisseur's relish of the great seductress at work—and Enobarbus goes with Antony too far to turn back.

Antony proceeds with a set will to defy the world, to reassure himself of his ability to do so. Plainly he is driven by a demon of necessity. There is something fatal in his determination, which leaves him only reckless of common sense whilst at the same time he cannot be indifferent to his fate. Now that he has ended the long enchanted sojourn his utterances tend to wistfulness. This comes out too in his unworthy errors of judgement, in which he has always to recognize an inexpugnable perversity necessary to his pride. He behaves like a man who knows he is going to be killed, the foolishness of whose judgement actually stimulates him and assures him that in this love he is seriously up against things. Thus the Soothsayer, like the Witches in *Macbeth*, predicts only what is inevitable in his soul—what in fact he determines shall be: he will not alter his purposes to ward off Caesar. Let Caesar win, if that is how the world is constituted: which defiance constitutes Antony's grasp on reality. Tragically, the decision that " I' th' East my pleasure lies " is tantamount to " and let come on me what will ". The material upon which his sad, defiant will is to work is the Cleopatra, lisless, craving, and self-centred, of the followng Scene.

Waited on by Charmian Cleopatra deeply expects, desires and waits on Antony's next move, cultivating her satisfaction so as to sate and leave herself prepared for nothing and anything. She luxuriates in sensual discontent, dramatizing her

deprivation so as to exacerbate and enjoy it and thus the knowledge that Antony is tied to her:

> I'll none now,
> Give me mine angle, we'll to th' river: there,
> My music playing far off, I will betray
> Tawny-finned fishes; my bended hook shall pierce
> Their slimy jaws, and as I draw them up,
> I'll think them every one an Antony,
> And say, "Ah, ha! you're caught."

Full of herself and of her past achievement—"That time—
O times!"—when the long-awaited messenger appears it is
"<Ram> thou thy fruitful tidings in mine ears," accom-
panied by an elaborate performance to delay any such haste
until she has wrought herself to a pitch of excited anticipation,
suspended between rapture and horror, waiting to be pushed
one way or the other. The to-do she creates in advance of any
inkling of the man's sorry tale, becoming to perfection the
fickle, dangerous queen, is pure hope and expectation and
desire, of something evermore about to be. In her soul she has
faith that some shock will thrill and set her wildly off she
knows not whither—she trusts the absent Antony so far. And:

> I do not like "But yet," it does allay
> The good precedence; fie upon "But yet"!
> "But yet" is as a gaoler to bring forth
> Some monstrous malefactor:

she knows what he is going to say. So when she is thrillingly,
oh so horribly and excitingly confirmed in her anticipation,
far from being put out of countenance, cast down, crushed,
or made supremely indifferent because Antony has calmly
gone and married someone else, she is wrought to an exquisite
pitch of cultivated excitement and dramatic dismay. It is
comical to behold: "I am pale, Charmian": she is furious
perfectly to form, unsurprised, and beautifully, extravagantly
wild:

What say you?
[*strikes him again*] Hence,
Horrible villain! or I'll spurn thine eyes
Like balls before me; I'll unhair thy head,
[*she hales him up and down*]
Thou shalt be whipped with wire, and stewed in brine,
Smarting in ling'ring pickle.

It is magnificent, and very funny, she is so reliable and up to it. Her insistent " He is married?", to overbear the messenger and make the greatest dramatic capital of his fear, is pure theatre, for of course were she let down by Antony what interest would she have in terrifying a minion? Whatever Antony's intention in marrying Octavia he is understood by Cleopatra to be paying her out with the vigour her gross satisfaction demands. Really her faith keeps her undaunted, so that she knows what is to be done in a moment: " Bring me word quickly." Her rage is unfeigned yet leaves her essentially intact, within her cultivation; far from consulting her personal happiness or estimating her chances for the future she looks immediately to find her ground so that she can rise to Antony's challenge. This is the love-game played for final stakes, histrionic but never faltering—even here Cleopatra's demeanour is perfect:

In praising Antony, I have dispraised Caesar.
Charmian. Many times, madam.
Cleopatra.   I am paid for 't now.

Such satisfaction! Her proprietorship of Antony and sedulous disregard of what he might do to smash it so fully answered! To discover the charms of Octavia has of course nothing to do with any sense of defeat; enacting her dreadful change before the audience of Charmian, devotee of her cult, she begins now to set the *scenario* required for Antony's altered status with her—" my man of men " now in an unknown sense:

Though he be painted one way like a Gorgon,
The other way 's a Mars.

Rueful, happy Cleopatra!

> Pity me, Charmian,
> But do not speak to me.

Desolate, she never assumes but that he and she are face to face
in the royal scrap of love, and is incapable of spite.

Cleopatra's faith that Antony is nowhere but at grips with
her in his marriage to Octavia is shown to be justified by
Antony's masterful despatch of his Roman affairs. Pompey is
surprised and utterly defeated in the pride of his ambition:
the mere presence of Antony has him explaining himself:

> I meant
> To scourge th' ingratitude that despiteful Rome
> Cast on my noble father.

What is the use of having meant to have ... ? He is neutralized, and his followers are not pleased. The bent of Antony's
thoughts when they greet shows why Antony has so quelled
Pompey's spirit, who believed but a moment before that " the
people love me ":

> I did not think, sir, to have met you here.
> *Antony.* The beds i' th' East are soft; and thanks to you,
> That called me timelier than my purpose hither;
> For I have gained by it.

Gained not Octavia or security, but the upper hand i' th' East;
his soldiership: and a *casus belli* for the inevitable contest with
Caesar, however he may congratulate himself on having
pulled off a political *coup* in the marriage with Octavia and
so proved his capacity for " Roman " action unimpaired.
Antony's sights are set on distant matters, and so despite his
liking for Pompey he wants him disarmed and out of the way
quite as much as Lepidus and Caesar do. He is not enough
" present to the present matter " for its own sake to lament for
Pompey that his treaty is a " sell-out ". Pompey, his belief in
his ambition broken under the great wheel of Antony's policy,
tries to be a common soldier again and greets Enobarbus as a

comrade in arms; but Caesar, once having been challenged by
him, has him eliminated as soon as he decently can. During
the celebration on board ship Pompey fights shy of the chance
to secure his first object at a single, dishonourable stroke, but
is shown even so to be merely in disguise pretending to be a
simple soldier ("Ah, this thou should'st have done, / And
not have spoke on 't! In me 'tis villainy; / In thee 't had been
good service "). It casts a sinister light on Antony's revels and
Caesar's, showing by implicit contrast (it is the purport of the
scene) the concentrated, watchful souls of both, their aptitude
for power and the necessity to be dangerous that accompanies
it. This quality in Antony is underlined in the following
scene, during which his lieutenant, Ventidius, is shown to be
afraid to challenge his chief's prowess in war. Yet it is the
politically able, dangerous Antony whom Caesar defeats.
Antony is never free like Enobarbus to " enjoy his plainness ",
to mock the flattering Lepidus, for example, but is perpetually
bound to make the running lest his world overtake and crush
him.

The sentiments Antony is prone to are all connected with
his further purposes, to secure his independence and possess
Cleopatra on terms possible for him; as she understands.
When the triumvirs part, a peculiarly real feeling of well-
wishing accompanies their guardedness, as of the unexpressed
mutual acknowledgement of adversaries. Things are not to
be the same again; there is a savour of change; sorrow, and
apprehension of an unknown issue; an emotional pause:

Antony.   Come, sir, come;
   I 'll wrestle with you in my strength of love:
   And give you to the gods.
Caesar.   Adieu; be happy!

Antony's and Caesar's feelings—the purport of the marriage
being plain—cause Enobarbus amusement: " That year indeed
he was troubled with a rheum;/ What willingly he did con-
found he wailed, / Believe 't, till I wept too." But Antony is far
from concealing a cynicism like Enobarbus's under a serious
aspect—he begins a real journey here; the marriage is as serious

as his ultimate fate and the slightly surprising, real emotion in the leave-taking betrays the necessity underlying his policy.

Antony and Caesar look seriously beyond the cynical present and their subordinates can only shake their heads and wonder. In contrast Cleopatra, also looking to the future, cultivates an elaborate comedy of grief reassuring to her artistic supremacy after her reversal. She demands, and is satisfied by, an arch flattery which really signifies no more than the need to feel herself still the priestess of Love's mysteries, mistress of her wiles:

Charmian. A proper man.
Cleopatra. Indeed, he is so: I repent me much
    That so I harried him. Why, methinks, by him,
    This creature's no such thing.
Charmian.   Nothing, madam.
Cleopatra. The man hath seen some majesty, and should
                                 know.
Charmian. Hath he seen majesty? Isis else defend,
    And serving you so long!

Cleopatra's artificiality asks for, and gets, artificiality, signalling that her style is unimpaired and her power to invent, and to set the tone of her court, stands undaunted. Undeceived, she is filled with belief in herself as a match for any Mark Antony whatsoever.

Despite his intention to be a capable Roman and also to keep Cleopatra as his mistress Antony never behaves as though he thinks any less than his match of her, for soon Octavia has his leave to leave and, cursing Caesar's interference with his plans, he returns to her when she " nods " or rather writes as both knew he eventually would. His hand forced, he makes the flaunting display in Alexandria his great, reckless stand, for Cleopatra and against Rome, and really lets himself in for her this time, who

    In th'habiliments of the goddess Isis
    That day appeared.

Cleopatra crossed, furious and desolate, is in a trice the incarnate goddess, with the Roman sternly reckless at her side. A remarkable rally? She never prepared for anything different. Her anguish was suffered with an anticipatory chuckle and a sidelong look, returned by Charmian. Antony is far gone: " His sons he there proclaimed the kings of kings." Why not? But his face was surely set, whilst hers was serene.

When Octavia turns up in Rome unattended it offends Caesar's sense of propriety and he delivers an address on the matter: " the trees by th' way / Should have borne men, and expectation fainted *&c.*" Then it remains only to announce the *casus belli*:

> He hath given his empire
> Up to a whore, who now are levying ...

... a lot of native chiefs. His relish, mouthing the outlandish names of Antony's exotic allies, smacks of self-satisfaction, as does his disapprobation of Antony defying Rome to immolate himself on his pride. That the Eastern kings defy Rome confirms Caesar in his impeccable sense of right, and he opposes the colonial governor who has " gone native", feeling the weight of all civilization at his back. His words of reassurance to Octavia must be the most unconsciously revealing in the play:

> Be you not troubled with the time, which drives
> O'er your content these strong necessities,
> But let determined things to destiny
> Hold unbewailed their way.

The triumph instilled into Caesar by Antony's reckless initiative gives the lie to this historical materialism; success completely convinces Caesar that his use of his sister to bring down his enemy is pure historical necessity. Antony, of course, " married but his occasion " in Octavia, but then he does not dissimulate ambition under a conviction of serving the inevitable ends of empire. The great, " opposeless " régime whose spirit Caesar would embody becomes a lie in him as the passion to overcome and vanquish his temperamental opposite and vindicate himself possesses him. It was this that put the yearning into his apostrophe to Antony to "leave thy lascivious wassails", and it now exultantly informs his statement to Octavia that "the high gods, / To do you justice, make his ministers / Of us and those that love you." Caesar triumphs, and Maecenas's remark that Antony has given "his potent regiment to a trull" exhibits just the gloating, pitying tone you begin now to hear from Caesar himself.

Even so, he is fascinated by and half admires the elder man's single desire about which he is so scornful. His attraction towards Antony, for Caesar is essentially not scornful or indifferent to him but absorbed, explains his power over him; for Antony is hardly aware of Caesar but as a hurdle between him and his desire, and is therefore continually surprised by his certain despatch ("Is it not strange, Canidius?", "You have heard on't, sweet?"). Antony defies not Caesar but Fortune: that gives Caesar his conviction of "strong necessities". Antony thinking to meet him and settle it on a personal level shows himself befogged: "Canidius, we / Will fight with him by sea ... For that he dares us to it." Enobarbus tries to tell him this when he admonishes him, "you therein throw away / The absolute soldiership you have by land ... leave unexecuted / Your own renowned knowledge, quite forego / The way which promises assurance, and / Give up yourself merely to chance and hazard / From firm security." Specifically to fly in the face of security becomes a fixed idea with Antony when necessity bedazzles his judgement, reducing his will from servant of his desire to a motor driving him. He cannot any longer anticipate Caesar because of his necessity to be singlemindedly or not at all "for love". That disabling pride disconnects him from reality and leaves him wondering. But it is a pride and not a fatuity and somehow Caesar recognizes that it has to be—Caesar's behaviour is the form of his knowledge; and his supremacy overcomes Antony with wonder.

The soldier who bids Antony fight by land speaks to him man to man in the way Antony has always relied upon: and he turns away, unable to listen to it. "We are women's men" is half true but the foolishness is his devotion, Antony's defiant commitment to the love of Cleopatra in reaction from the eternal dream of dalliance. Spectacular as ever, Cleopatra arouses a kind of distraught admiration even in the fantasia at Actium: "The breese upon her, like a cow in June!— / Hoists sails and flies." The soldiers' exasperation with Antony can only be pretty final—" the noble ruin of her magic "; but then the episode is full of her magic, and his allowance of Cleopatra's fantasy to command from the flagship is his devotion to it. Being far gone he becomes a menace, love undoes him and makes him active, doing, and a threat to the peace of the world.

Feeling the irresistible current bear him to destruction, Antony pathetically appeals to his friends' esteem for him. He invites them to leave him to his ruin, but his intimacy with them only shows his dependence on their sympathy:

> Hark! the land bids me tread no more upon 't—
> It is ashamed to bear me. Friends, come hither:
> I am so lated in the world that I
> Have lost my way for ever.

The falling cadence of dismay conveys not shame but regret, yearning for his old esteem as he floats on whither he will not return. Always the wish to keep the personal connection with his men through generosity and mutual regard, never to betray his comradeship whatever may befall him personally—and to make his friends weep, holds off blame: "Pray you, look not sad." He turns all their unanswerable judgement to tears; he appeals through their scorn to their sympathy; he says, "Let that be left / Which leaves itself," but assumes their good wishes. Temporarily abashed by his fortunes, Antony assumes the loyalty of his followers to his good faith as Cleopatra assumes his, and her court's, devotion to Love:

> Leave me, I pray, a little: pray you now,
> Nay, do so; for indeed I have lost command,
> Therefore I pray you: I'll see you by and by.

To beg their forgiveness or to brow-beat them does not occur to him. He shoulders his own defeat as for all, and is sorry only that he cannot give his men victory rather than treasure and a safe passage. Generous in defeat, yet he blames Cleopatra that somehow his red blood is overwhelmed by the Caesarian lymph:

> Egypt, thou knew'st too well
> My heart was to thy rudder tied by th' strings,
> And thou should'st tow me after: o'er my spirit
> Thy full supremacy thou knew'st, and that
> Thy beck might from the bidding of the gods
> Command me.

It was his will that she should have her way and fight alongside him; and now she begs his pardon, no longer mocking but generous and attentive to his sacrifice for them. It is not her aim to reduce him to wistfulness and defeat; her ridiculous, splendidly unconsidered gesture was to encourage them both, as indeed his reckless allowance of it acknowledged. They are fools unto themselves, and discover a new, sympathetic intimacy after the fight: "Love, I am full of lead." Comforted with that solace (although solace was no more the aim than was defeat at Actium), Antony absurdly sends his schoolmaster to beg that he may be let live "a private man in Athens". In this he shows his indifference as to whether Caesar takes it as conciliation or an insult—whereupon Caesar ignorantly despatches a man to entice Cleopatra off.

With Cleopatra it is a genuine question, "Is Antony or we in fault for this?" She wants to know, for seeing Antony's peculiarly serious dismay she discovers a new role for herself, one strange to her majestic assumption. Enobarbus's judgement is absolute and unanswerable:

> Antony only, that would make his will
> Lord of his reason. What though you fled
> From that great face of war, whose several ranges
> Frighted each other, why should he follow?

Antony's behaviour was not regal; nor is his challenge to meet Caesar in a duel. His manhood, baffled in itself, becomes strident and unable, the real evidence of his defeat.

Enobarbus resolves to leave him, not for his fortunes' decline, but for his disintegration as a man of responsible power.

Enobarbus reconciles himself to losing a master; Cleopatra grows superb in devotion, devastating in the pride of her love. She receives Thidias—" Go on: right royal "—with a display of such consummate irony Antony cannot himself for a long time believe what she is at, how she is inspired now to concentrate all her gifts to his defence, no longer to provoke and madden him but to stand up for him:

> Say to great Caesar this: in deputation
> I kiss his conqu'ring hand: tell him, I am prompt
> To lay my crown at 's feet, and there to kneel:
> Tell him, from his all-obeying breath I hear
> The doom of Egypt ... .

He accuses her of treachery; she is too far before him. Only Enobarbus, the enthusiast for her " infinite variety ", understands the impossibility of Cleopatra's being anything but dangerous in giving Caesar's man her " bluest veins " to kiss. The masterpiece of devoted mockery of Antony's enemies which he witnesses in this humour of the Queen clinches his certitude that Antony cannot be much longer for this world. (If that's where Cleopatra is ... .) Caesar simply does not exist after this superb repulse. His ignorant confidence that he knows where Cleopatra is tells Cleopatra all she needs to know about Caesar in order to defeat his intentions for her when she falls into his hands. On being rewarded only by Antony's suspicious scorn ("she here—what's her name / Since she was Cleopatra?") she responds with but a forbearing protestation of her loyalty to him, understanding the hardness for Antony to achieve her serenity. The Cleopatra of Acts I and II, countered in all her wilful vanity, is inspired now in love; no longer a game, it fills her with masterful certitude. Antony is as slow to come up with her as he was then ("How, my love?")—only with even better reason: now she is too serene for their peace. He seems to allow that she may be somewhere ahead of him, demanding and resting satisfied with her vigorous pledge of loyalty. Even so, his " for

I have savage cause" is more than a self-excusing instance of
" I told him of myself, which was as much / As to have asked
him pardon." He is savage against his fate, and against her
more particularly as her forbearing to deny what he accuses
her of here with characteristic Cleopatrian joy is ominous.

Antony rages against his stars half from a real sense of
injustice, half from a wish to put the blame firmly there and
resist Cleopatra's new sympathy, for he is baffled and behind-
hand in his love:

> He makes me angry,
> And at this time most easy 't is to do 't:
> When my good stars that were my former guides
> Have empty left their orbs and shot their fires
> Into th' abysm of hell.

For unless the gods have got it in for him, why is he about to
be trounced by the boy Caesar? Is it because he is a woman's
man? It troubles him that she should suddenly seem to want
to soothe him. He does not seek a different, sympathetic Cleopatra, but needs on the contrary to feel the antagonism of the
" right gypsy ", the strong magic that explains his decline in a
way acceptable to honour. But he has her with him, un-
questioning. He angles after the old reassurance:

> Alack, our terrene moon
> Is now eclipsed:

Cleopatra, that is, favouring Caesar's man. The invitation to
her violently to deny the implication is met, however, by a
vehement demonstration of loyalty: "Ah, dear, if I be so, /
From my cold heart let heaven engender hail &c." He declares
himself " satisfied "—presumably that at least she does not
quarrel with his passion, even if it is disconcerting if she
shares it.

More than " satisfied ", Antony is in heart again—" Dost
thou hear, lady?"—and Cleopatra, satisfied that he does not
wait on her, receives his determinations with joy, for they
assure her confidence of fulfilment. In his " I will be treble-
sinewed, hearted, breathed" she hears only the pledge of faith,

Antony all for love, which (dissociated from actuality as he may be) completes her in her great desire for them both to defeat the world in a glorious death. The more recklessly determined on behalf of them both he becomes the more the fatality of their passion itself inspires her. Enobarbus sees the " diminution in our captain's brain "—becomes able to call it that—only as he comes to understand Cleopatra's inspiration; that the one is the condition of the other; and that in them both he is betrayed. His loyalty to Antony and admiration of Cleopatra and of what Antony and she are making together leaves him with the choice of suicidal loyalty or desertion. Enobarbus's crisis comes from Antony's, which it parallels; deserting (as Antony tragically deserts honour) he dies the death imposed by an inevitable dishonour. Antony suffers the anguish of dishonour as he imposes this dishonour on his friend and lieutenant. But was he, having loved Cleopatra, to have " pulled himself together "? Or languished in Egypt for ever her paramour? Antony is his friend's betrayer, and that is tragic.

Antony's disorientation makes Caesar a satisfied man: " Let the old ruffian know ... ." He permits himself the joke of letting Antony's own deserters finish him off; and a princely gesture: " Feast the army ... they have earned the waste." Finding himself with the upper hand he becomes condescending, "Poor Antony!", showing an unhandsome disapprobation, humourless and vindictive, which redounds upon his righteousness. The play's judgement upon Antony's quite unarguable disgrace is complex, and makes us wonder at what waxes as Antony wanes.

Antony's instinct to make a scene has him making his subordinates weep, with " may be it is the period of your duty." He disclaims the intention but sounds defeated in anticipation:

> I hope well of tomorrow, and will lead you
> Where rather I'll expect victorious life
> Than death and honour. Let's to supper, come,
> And drown consideration.

During his Last Supper his god leaves him and, " lated in the

world ", he is left to contend with death armed solely with
Cleopatra's desire to make death proud. The prospect of battle
elates him and fills him—perhaps, for his clearer sight of what
must be, more poignantly than Othello is filled—with the
liberty of martial execution. Arming, he anticipates the day
with wry humour:

Cleopatra.   Nay, I 'll help too.
        What 's this for?
Antony.   Ah, let be! thou art
        The armourer of my heart: false, false: this, this.
Cleopatra. Sooth, la, I 'll help: thus it must be.
Antony.   Well, well,
        We shall thrive now.

The defection of Enobarbus, prelude to the most painful scene
in the play, his death of a broken heart, follows remorselessly
upon Antony's sniffing the day's air, destroying even that wry
happiness by insisting on the inexpugnable irresponsibility of
his valour. Enobarbus is his friend. On the threshold of battle
Antony can only reproach his " fortunes " with having " corrupted honest men "; whereupon he gratifies his magnanimity
with a characteristic gesture of largesse—the fatal one. It
escapes him that if " I ", not " my fortunes ", had " corrupted
honest men ", " I " could not have " subscribed " a letter of
forgiveness. Antony is blind, and believes that Enobarbus is
the only betrayer, whom he must forgive. This deep dissociation of his spirit from his judgement corresponds not acci-
dentally with a new vindictiveness in his enemy: " Our will is
Antony be took alive." That is Caesar's real intention now
that he perceives that Antony is lost; not to give peace—" The
time of universal peace is near "—but to triumph. His passion
is now to vanquish and crow; Antony's willing struggle in
Cleopatra's " strong toil of grace " has put it in him. For all
that his temper is foreign to Antony's he despises his desire
and cannot ignore it, for it compels him to annihilate it and
smile in superiority with " the time of universal peace is near."
        The recurring cadence of dismay that accompanies all that

is glorious in the play is resolved in Enobarbus's accusation of himself of having done the wrong thing by Antony:

> I have done ill,
> Of which I do accuse myself so sorely
> That I will joy no more.

When Antony falls into a similar intonation—which it is characteristic of him to do—it is from sentimental regret for simpler times. But Enobarbus is pronouncing his own last judgement. He is unable to live with himself any more. This is the end of sentimental evasion, and to Antony's shame the finality comes not with his own but with his friend's betrayal of faith. When Antony breaks Enobarbus's heart with his largesse and magnanimous forgiveness, even though these are of the essence of the man and perfectly sincere, even self-accusatory, generosity itself becomes a lie, itself unforgiveable. He cannot stop to feel how Enobarbus must feel receiving his gifts and good wishes, for the generosity is not false but most true, most essentially Antony. The imperious need which has him attracting his followers' sympathy for his fallen fortunes has this consequence:

> No, I will go seek
> Some ditch wherein to die; the foul'st best fits
> My latter part of life:

which, hopelessly, fatally wrong, is love's doing. For Enobarbus is not wrong about his master's generous spirit, who in victory is filled with admiration for his soldiers and gratitude:

> I thank you all,
> For doughty-handed are you, and have fought
> Not as you served the cause, but as 't had been
> Each man's like mine; you have shown all Hectors.

He hates himself that he is driven to fail such magnanimity (which, unbearably, Antony unintentionally rubs in)—and yet, it is hopeless.

Antony gives his men the laurels and Cleopatra his joy, which she accepts with joy despite her realistic "Then Antony,

but now ... ." For, supremely happy in the achievement of
the hour, the consequences notwithstanding (precisely), he
affirms his pledge to her and their mutual pledge to an aristo-
cratic sufficiency. For the moving gift of his content she
renders him lordship:

> Lord of lords!
> O infinite virtue, comest thou smiling from
> The world's great snare uncaught?

These words, moving because they convey her supreme happiness in her gift, and because that happiness and these words are
pure will, Cleopatra's sheer courage of her determination,
make his abandoned valour the accomplishment he strives
after, and an authentic gesture of love. Confirming his gesture
by her brave declaration, she is herself inspired with pure faith
in the hour. Her disregard of tomorrow, originally only her
grand style, is wrought now by love into the faith in which she
moves to make love eternal. Her poetry from here to the end
makes clear and true the inspiration that his donation body
and soul to her has made of her "infinite variety"; its consummation is to be its immolation on the altar of Love.
Antony's lesser tragedy is the necessary condition of her
greater. His love now given her freely on account of no wiles
of hers, his tragedy bears witness to the necessity which is
Cleopatra's incomparable nature as Enobarbus's tragedy bears
witness to Antony's. His triumph—

> O thou day o' th' world,
> Chain mine armed neck; leap thou, attire and all,
> Though proof of harness to my heart, and there
> Ride on the pants triumphing!

—at once becomes pathetic by association with the indulgence
of "Trumpeters, / With brazen din blast you the city's ear";
but it is at once hopeless and their deepest union, their triumph
in each other.

In this play's mode of remorseless alternation between belief
and actuality the quiet watch of the sentries establishes upon
that joyous affirmation, with Shakespearean economy, the
contrary motion of fate:

> the night
> Is shiny, and they say we shall embattle
> By th' second hour i' th' morn.

The stars glisten imminently over the unapprehensive soldiers over whom with their masters fate impends. By similarly associating the impersonal heavens with human life Enobarbus, taking his leave of life, addresses the moon, "Sovereign mistress of true melancholy"; for the "terrene moon" on whose account Antony challenges his fate is as much the light of his life, and *via* his attachment to Antony, of his death as well. By calling the moon to witness, Enobarbus signifies his own submission to that unapproachable, remote quality Cleopatra has at the centre of her "infinitely various" personality, the infinity itself, the fact that she cannot be caught and finally known, being maddening and irresistible whether it attract or repel. He refers himself to the essential, the fatal Cleopatra for the judgement of the fault for which he wishes no longer to live ("throw my heart / Against the flint and hardness of my fault") and his devotion to her hands Antony too over to his death. Enobarbus throws himself upon the judgement of the remote moon, and thus upon all that Cleopatra essentially is; and we detest Antony's imposition upon his friend even as we see in the seriousness of Enobarbus's remorse, his deathly wish to be judged only by her, the inevitability and fatality of love. Enobarbus cannot pardon his own fault, because it is Antony he has failed—not the dishonour but the deep realization this brings of the character of the man he fails makes him hate his life with wholly original seriousness. Antony is as far gone as this unbearable consequence. The play insists on it, alternating scenes of the one's progress to death in a ditch with scenes of the other's exalted faith in the sufficiency of the day. But Antony's state of hopeless unreason is the condition of his achievement for Cleopatra; of his being for an hour "uncaught"; of his defeating the world—to that extent.

Antony. I would they 'ld fight i' th' fire or i' th' air;
     We 'ld fight there too ... .
Caesar.   ... we will be still by land. .

When the inevitable defeat occurs he cannot help himself and blames Cleopatra, although not deeply believing she can have gone behind his back and dealt with Thidias now. But his fortunes are perverse past bearing because of the tragic lie of his indifference to the world. He endeavours to blast her, its cause, from his mind with abuse and unfair accusation, to prevent himself from examining his mind, for to do so would be to see that he must go with her to the bitter end. It serves a need of his manhood paramount and undeniable which, once propitiated, leaves him free to follow his fortunes without rancour (albeit without any great clarity):

> The hearts
> That spanieled me at heels, to whom I gave
> Their wishes, do discandy, melt their sweets
> On blossoming Caesar; and this pine is barked,
> That overtopped them all. Betrayed I am.
> O this false soul of Egypt! this grave charm—
> Whose bosom was my crownet, my chief end—
> Like a right gypsy hath at fast and loose
> Beguiled me to the very heart of loss.

Is the exculpating picture really any more realistic than his blame of his "fortunes": "O, my fortunes have / Corrupted honest men"? Somewhere he knows himself innerly wrong, lost in his deepest passion, and his dudgeon and his remorse alike repudiate the blame. Blaming other people he is not honest, nevertheless the cry for his hopeless plight to be seen is as undeniable as Lear's false blame of the gods. Antony suffers from the futility of his rage as Lear does: it hurts him because he is by nature the opposite of a vain or an impotent man. If his intentions are less admirable than Lear's, lack their redemptory cast, still like Lear's his pain is his and not to be denied. Cleopatra wisely leaves him to come to some realization of her and of what she has to do through his sufferings, for what he has to do for her and them tears him apart, and her presence were hardly to be borne. He accuses her of treachery, but as he fights her "grave charm" it only tangles him the more.

Such is her perfect assumption, his resistance merely puzzles her: "Why is my lord enraged against his love?" She has had once already to inquire, gently, "Not know me yet?" The mischievous intention in that implicitly refers him to their vaunting intimacy when it was "Lord of lords" and all fine love-language between them, and asks Antony to come up with her now and not take his loss as the end of the world. The intimacy assumes all; the assumption in the intimacy makes all that is assumed inevitably to be the case. To contradict her would not only be to repudiate all that Cleopatra now openly and invitingly shows herself to be, but also to go back on all that he has said and done with her to make her thus. What she is now they have both made. He knows the gypsy in her which is her magic, and bucks against his submission to it; he who desired it will not have it—he cannot have it; it goes against his nature, after all, to set at naught the judgement of the world. That is his fight and she cannot help him. There is more yet which, when he has got over his rage at her as a "right gypsy", she will have still to show.

Meanwhile, determined to bring these developments to their conclusion—for he seriously needs to believe he can—Antony is filled with a dismissive grandiloquence like Hamlet's when he overcomes his distaste for violence enough to resolve to settle Rosencrantz and Guildenstern ("But I will delve one yard below their mines / And blow them at the moon"):

> The shirt of Nessus is upon me: teach me,
> Alcides, thou mine ancestor, thy rage:
> Let me lodge Lichas on the horns o' th' moon,
> And with those hands that grasped the heaviest club
> Subdue my worthiest self.

Like Hamlet he is not escaping into the posture of a tragic hero, but drawing himself up in the fashion native to him to meet the unknown "doom of Egypt" in following Cleopatra, whither he cannot see and moreover is determined no longer to ask.

This is pure Antony, and as ever it fills Cleopatra with the spirit of mischief. Her reaction to his rage is to appeal to her attendants for confirmation that she behaves with fitting cunning, to counter his passion as in the old dance:

> Help me, my women! O, he's more mad
> Than Telamon for his shield; the boar of Thessaly
> Was never so embossed.

Her freakish talk reveals her delight; she takes up Charmian's cry, "To th' monument," and leaps to embrace the idea and make it her own like some Natasha Rostova. Antony's dangerous spleen only inspires her to circumvent him and lead him a merry dance. But when he has finished moaning and storming against necessity and committing himself to the " gypsy ", he suffers a vision of the insubstantiality of " this compound mass " (Hamlet), of the evanescence of all substantial reality, which is an insight into the essential Cleopatra in her ultimate, transcendently sensual end:

> Sometimes we see a cloud that's dragonish,
> A vapour sometimes like a bear or lion,
> A towered citadel, a pendent rock,
> A forked mountain, or blue promontory
> With trees upon't, that nod unto the world
> And mock our eyes with air: thou hast seen these signs;
> They are black Vesper's pageants.

Eros.   Ay, my lord.
Antony. That which is now a horse, even with a thought
>   The rack dislimns, and makes it indistinct
>   As water is in water.

Realized with the force and beauty of his imagination's possession of the world's beauty as " pageants " heralding night and darkness, this constitutes—Cleopatra's exaltation of the body and the life in the senses to godhead being yet to come— a deep commitment to the unknown.

Antony bids a farewell to arms with obvious relief, and is pathetic in his belief that, dying the soldier's death, he overtakes Cleopatra. His wishful fancy of overhauling her and, hand in hand, astonishing Hades, is too easily had to be true and just shows him to be at the command of whatever contingency may now present itself; it is a beauty devoutly to be wished but unreal compared with the force of his poetry of loss:

> Where souls do couch on flowers, we'll hand in hand,
> And with our sprightly port make the ghosts gaze.

The desire is real enough, for one intention is now as good as another: the will has all gone into dreams, earnest and unmeaning. He doesn't want to kick against the pricks any more, and he must have Cleopatra ... here are terms upon which to meet her. To be absolute for death! (believing her, wrongly, to be dead):

> Since Cleopatra died [five minutes?]
> I have lived in such dishonour that the gods
> Detest my baseness.

Readily assuming his "baseness", by which he means that he lags behind Cleopatra, he only displays his hankering to end his actual dishonour. The thought of her fills his mind and drives from his thought all else but the desire to catch her and step with her into death, or wherever it may be. She has put death into his mind by her high-spirited subterfuge, in which he believes immediately: for nothing she can do can now surprise him. His decision to die is nevertheless moving for the witness the relief in it bears to the intolerable persistence of love towards its end, and for the gratitude:

> but I will be
> A bridegroom in my death, and run into 't
> As to a lover's bed.

How the imagined sacrifice to what he takes for her desire is embraced! And how Antony is reproached in the very act by a real sacrifice! Eros's suicide relentlessly shows Antony's for the unmeaning resolve it is; shows the pathos of a death that has no necessary character with relation to Antony's deepest

truth, for all his intention that it should bring matters to a
triumphantly final close. He takes his life with courage, but
his profound soul is meanwhile unengaged with the fancy he
is enacting with all his will to make the ghosts gaze. Yet the
difficulty for Antony to persist redeems the intention, and as he
is a fool he is true.

He is a fool, though, with the finality of self-murder. That
breaks the last barrier of illusion, and when he hears that
Cleopatra is still alive he does not groan, for he is hers and
anything she does belongs to her and is her: "When did she
send thee?" His death?

> do not please sharp fate
> To grace it with your sorrows: bid that welcome
> Which seems to punish us, and we punish it
> Seeming to bear it lightly. Take me up.

We have heard that tone before, it is the vaunting love-
language of Antony and Cleopatra. Resuming the old brave
indifference he signals that he understands that he has "come
through", caught up with her at last, and is to die her hero.
Thus remorse is ever defeated, and in his being Antony is not
ashamed, but only self-deprecating for his incapacity and dependence, so that the regretful intonation lingers in his re-
quest to his attendants: "I have led you oft, carry me now,
good friends, / And have my thanks for all"—coloured by
confidence that his thanks are still currency.

Cleopatra engineers Antony's death, which is as she wills it:

> All strange and terrible events are welcome,
> But comforts we despise; our size of sorrow,
> Proportioned to our cause, must be as great
> As that which makes it.
> How now! is he dead?

Just what is she warning her attendants to prepare their
sorrow to fit? That Antony would follow her into death was
her last faith, and having on an inspiration put it into his

mind she expects him to follow wherever he believes her to
have led. Her supreme creation is thus achieved by a characteristic Cleopatrian gambol, spontaneous and unintended, yet
deeply desired; for she knows of his death—her paean of
praise is ready on her lips for the splendid conclusion:

> O sun,
> Burn the great sphere thou mov'st in! darkling stand
> The varying shore o'th' world. O Antony,
> Antony, Antony! Help, Charmian, help, Iras, help;
> Help, friends below, let's draw him hither ...
> So should it be, that none but Antony
> Should conquer Antony, but woe 'tis so!

The supreme attraction of "our terrene moon" is to this
death and Antony does finally occasion her that pride.

Jealous of her achievement, she becomes touchingly fearful
that the world might thwart them in the end, spoiling the
gathering climax:

> I dare not, dear,
> Dear my lord, pardon: I dare not open,
> Lest I be taken.

Watchful and guarded, she hesitates to admit Antony to the
monument even whilst he might die: for the sake of what
they have made, caution is paramount even at their last farewell. Concentrated in her purpose, so that Antony naturally
defers to her, she works intently, talking the while:

> Here's sport indeed! How heavy weighs my lord!
> Our strength is all gone into heaviness;
> That makes the weight.

She says sport, but with his death upon them the time for sport
is past and she is anxious, serious and capable. Antony takes
his tone from her—the talk is to be all brave Antony and
Cleopatra, with no false note of archness:

> Yet come a little—
> Wishers were ever fools—O, come, come, come;
> And welcome, welcome! Die when thou hast lived,
> Quicken with kissing: had my lips that power,
> Thus would I wear them out.

"Wishers were ever fools"; Cleopatra's scornful belief in the moment, asserted here where they make their last embrace, gives Antony the death he desires to make, devoted to everything Cleopatra is. He assents to her characterization of his end, that death is inevitable but desire eternal in the living moment, and her business to cling to him and hurl defiance at the fates:

> No, let me speak, and let me rail so high,
> That the false huswife Fortune break her wheel,
> Provoked by my offence.

He shows he understands her intention by manfully advising her how to look after herself when he is gone: "Of Caesar seek your honour with your safety": advice without ground in the way things are. Nevertheless the last words of the consort of the fabulous queen are from pure loyalty to her and to them both, not self-regarding but apt as the finishing touch to their masterpiece (though inevitably consciously so). They are moving for Antony's perfect faith in them, the unasking devotion which culminates in this pathetically superb end:

> but please your thoughts
> In feeding them with those my former fortunes
> Wherein I lived ... the greatest prince o' th' world,
> The noblest ... and do now not basely die,
> Not cowardly put off my helmet to
> My countryman ... a Roman by a Roman
> Valiantly vanquished. Now my spirit is going,
> I can no more.

Moving too is Cleopatra's earnest loyalty in supporting him in the role, which still comes out unconsciously heartless:

"Noblest of men, woo't die?" No more acting, but perfect loyalty: but to what? "Shall I abide / In this dull world?": she declares her intention that he shall be immortalized in the triumph over death for which she yearns. Antony's triumph, his seriousness, inspires Cleopatra to complete her great task. Her picture of him is splendid and poignant in its passionate belief, its pure assumption that their eternity lies in glorious death:

> young boys and girls
> Are level now with men: the odds is gone,
> And there is nothing left remarkable
> Beneath the visiting moon.

Antony's truth came upon him as a bewildering vision of insubstantiality which was nevertheless powerless to deter him; Cleopatra, inspired, must wrest her truth from insubstantiality in giving herself willingly to the force and passion of love; whence the pathos of her lament. Her reality is the single desire for death—the final, obliterating unreality. Cleopatra's last seriousness, her disdainful pride of love, is her desire to have the ending of mortality.

The pride of love inspires her with passionate sincerity to vindicate her imagination of love, yet the "jewel" she jealously guards—Antony—she herself sacrifices:

> No more but e'en a woman, and commanded
> By such poor passion as the maid that milks
> And does the meanest chares. It were for me
> To throw my sceptre at the injurious gods,
> To tell them that this world did equal theirs
> Till they had stol'n our jewel.

She does not intend to cast her sceptre away in dudgeon, for her native pride bends to the one desire to surprise death in a famous and glorious assault in the name of Love, the love which Antony and Cleopatra shall apotheosize. Her native vivacity is inspired with its end:

> All's but naught;
> Patience is sottish, and impatience does
> Become a dog that's mad: then is it sin
> To rush into the secret house of death,
> Ere death dare come to us?

Is it? The question Shakespeare poses in Cleopatra's creation of a love that transcends, precisely, life is the one to which Hamlet's anguish answers for him, " Yes, it is sin," whilst his courage retorts, " No, it is the only noble course," when he goes to death in the pride of his love of the nobleness of life. Cleopatra braves death out in the splendid flesh—and her splendour is pathetic. The pathos runs right through the play, informing alike Antony's brave resolve to put an end to the dalliance of love and Cleopatra's sublime sacrifice in the last act.

When he actually vanquishes Antony Caesar takes himself by surprise: " in that name lay / A moiety of the world." A bit impressed despite himself, he is moved to praise Antony in a modest disclaimer. But his tone gives away his pride and pleasure; he is the peacemaker—" we do lance / Diseases in our bodies "—and in any case, " we could not stall together / In the whole world." Consoled, he begins to muse on Cleopatra, prey now himself to a curiosity to experience Antony's overweening pleasure in her—that is the motive of the betraying slip, " For her life in Rome / Would be eternal in our triumph." She, he means (the whore, the secret dealer with Thidias), who was too much for the great Antony.

What you actually hear from Cleopatra now has the force and beauty of her passionate abandonment to the strong central current flowing one way:

> Rather a ditch in Egypt
> Be gentle grave unto me! rather on Nilus' mud
> Lay me stark nak'd, and let the water-flies
> Blow me into abhorring!

The pure desire evident in this, coming where it does at the defeat of Antony and Cleopatra, is splendid and pathetic.

When Cleopatra pictures Antony to Dolabella as a kind of fabulous hero it is manifestly to find occasion in Dolabella's sensible demur to overbear " sense " with passion, reassuring her of the straight way to her destiny. For the " fact " whether " there was, or might be, such a man " as she has imagined Antony does not bear on the reality of their devotion. She toys with the fancy of such a man once more to know the creativity brought into being as the language of their love. That has not to do with the fancy's proving true: she can tease her seriousness about its truth in all seriousness.

" Eternity was in our lips and eyes " ceases to be a vaunting gesture and becomes death-defeating certitude. Cleopatra's eternity is so much the more pathetic than Antony's imaginations of what they might do (" make the ghosts gaze " &c.), which bear the relation to actuality that they allow him to suffer what they are doing and wear it out to the end, whereas she, who makes the running, only becomes dissociated from life and fit for death. Caesar threatens her children with death if she disobeys him. Immediately she sets about circumventing him, exercizing her art with all the old delight, quite indifferent to the fate of her family. When Caesar is about to leave her presence she brings forward a steward, Seleucus, whom she instructs to display an inventory: " Let him speak, my lord, / Upon his peril, that I have reserved / To myself nothing." With improbable effrontery Seleucus announces that she has reserved enough to purchase what she has declared. Caesar, amused to see that she is as cunning as they say, and gratified to note that she makes provision for the future and intends no suicide, is made a boy of.* Knowing he will believe in a cunning Cleopatra but not a complaisant one she flatters his knowledge of women: " My master, and my lord!" He thinks her to be winking at him to come to an understanding. She lets him think it while she instructs her people to prepare for her death.

For the victors she displays nothing but contempt:

Why, that's the way

* The point is made by John Dover Wilson in his introduction to the Cambridge edition of the play (p. xxxv).

To fool their preparation, and to conquer
Their most absurd intents.

Unworldly beyond the imagination of a Caesar, Cleopatra is filled with scornful resolution to make her vision a higher reality than " absurd " actuality, the mundane conquests of an emperor:

Now, Charmian!
Show me, my women, like a queen: go fetch
My best attires. I am again for Cydnus,
To meet Mark Antony.

The ecstasizing pose, unlike her acting of former times, is a deliberate gesture of devotion whose authenticity is owed to the desire in it—to consummate the " Cydnus " dream in death:

My resolution's placed, and I have nothing
Of woman in me. Now from head to foot
I am marble constant; now the fleeting moon
No planet is of mine.

The incantation to her essential spirit disdains to consider her mere humanity: " I have nothing of woman in me." Referred to nothing but the terms of her imagination of love's apotheosis, she puts off humanity as surely as Antony at his most reckless put off honour. In the courage of her self-election to godhead she becomes " marble ", beautiful substantial form, the spirit devoted eternally to the glory of the life in the flesh. The pathetic unreality (the indifference to the murder of her children, the fact that it is not a " baby " but a snake at her breast) attests to the desire. Her voluptuous triumph is tragic; beautifully Cleopatra, but poignant in the perfection, the finality of sensual passion. She tells herself joyfully what she feels and her triumph is purely of the unhindered will, of the liberty of all tragic heroism, to make an end:

Give me my robe, put on my crown, I have
Immortal longings in me. Now no more

The juice of Egypt's grape shall moist this lip.
Yare, yare, good Iras; quick. Methinks I hear
Antony call.

As she makes all this herself, with joy in the culmination of
her desire, her eager "methinks" is as wonderful as it is
poignantly unreal. Nevertheless to have come to make this
affirmation of her "immortal longings" is to have come to
make the end of her love as she has desired it, and she is here
inspired. The passionate desire here for death is Cleopatra's
ultimate truth, the culmination of such love as she has been
graced with for Antony, and as much what she is and must be
as Macbeth's drear dawning and resolution:

I am in blood
Stepped in so far that, should I wade no more,
Returning were as tedious as go o'er:
Strange things I have in head that will to hand,
Which must be acted ere they may be scanned.

Just as he is bound to do his now hateful will only in order to
accomplish nullity, so she is bound to her desire and to make
her death, though in the faith that her devotion is eternal.

The transubstantiation, ardently desired, is made possible
for her only by the embrace of the Mark Antony of their
mutual creation—"the greatest prince o'th'world": the
Mark Antony of Cleopatra's desire whom she goes to meet
with a devotion to their life-transcending love suiting his
courage to die her thrall:

I am fire and air; my other elements
I give to baser life.

The physical voluptuousness—

The stroke of death is as a lover's pinch,
Which hurts, and is desired

—makes her suicide a rough embrace of him, seizing and
enjoying: she makes a chase of it and pursues Iras into death,

with a pathetic devotion in the swoon of purely cultivated engrossedness:

> As sweet as balm, as soft as air, as gentle—
> O Antony!

For the voluptuous embrace and caught, yearning sigh of pure pleasure are her victory as they are her death. Charmian's lamentation, closing the corpse's eyes, "Downy windows close; / And golden Phoebus never be beheld / Of eyes again so royal!" is not misplaced, but the royalty lies there.